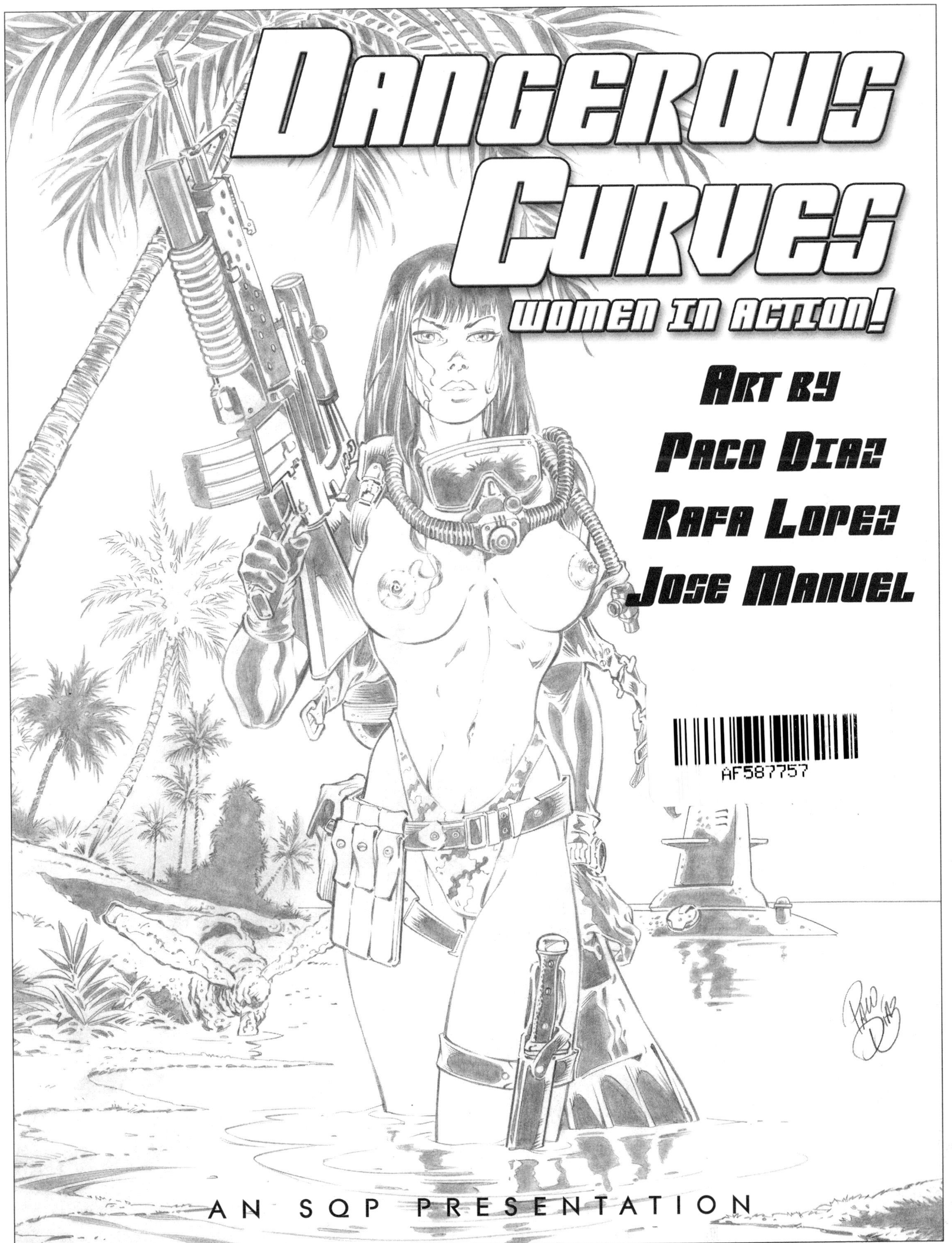
DANGEROUS
CURVES
WOMEN IN ACTION!
ART BY
PACO DIAZ
RAFA LOPEZ
JOSE MANUEL
AN SQP PRESENTATION

Dangerous Curves: Talented Artists

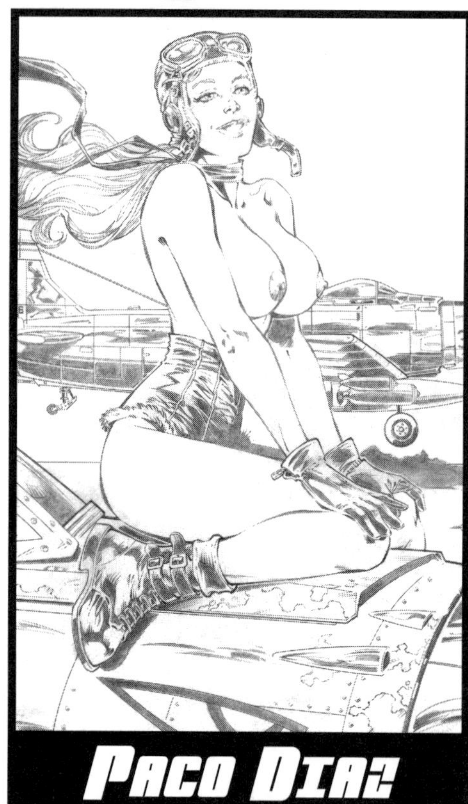

PACO DIAZ

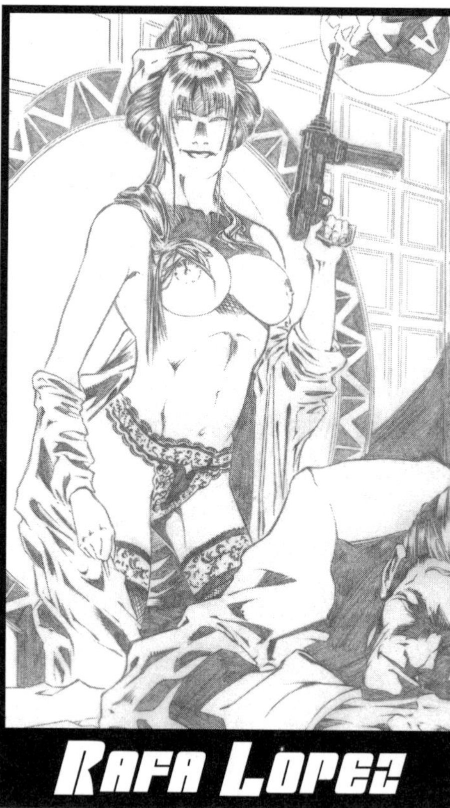

RAFA LOPEZ

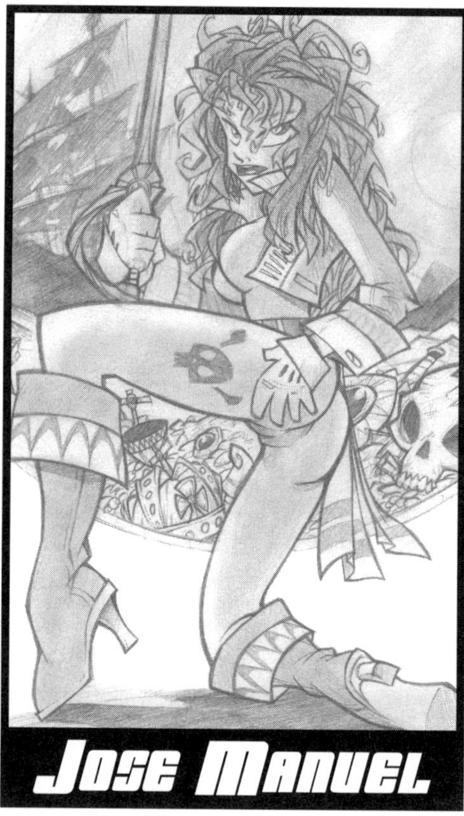

JOSE MANUEL

As anyone who watches the Nature Channel (or gets in a really nasty argument with their girlfriend) will tell you, the female is the most dangerous of genders. Sure, guys can pump and flex and train, but when it comes to out-and-out vicious, you're-dead-and-you-just-don't-know-it-yet, the ladies will take the prize ever time!

It was this concept rolling around in the head of Sal Quartuccio, el Presidente for life of SQP, as he was enjoying a business trip in sun-filled and beautiful Barcelona, Spain. Amid the myriad meetings and sightseeing, he was introduced to three young artists eager to showcase their abilities.

This young trio were Paco Diaz, Rafa Lopez, and Jose Manuel. Each had a penciling style that was unique, Diaz and Lopez having had the guidance of famed Barcelona Editor Xavier Marturet, while Manuel trained with the artist/editor Eduardo Alpuente.

Each artist was poised for assignment, pencil at hand on a blank slate. Sal thought this would be the perfect time to launch his little "deadly but delightful" project, so he laid the book out to them. Let's see what you can create with warrior women, female assassins, gun-toting terminators...basically hot babes who are deadly!

Fortunately, such concepts are universal, so the translations were hardly necessary. Soon, all three began producing an array of outrageous excess (which is something we're always in favor of!), with furious females ready to destroy any and all comers! Each in their own particular style, from realistic to fantasy, and each showing the fighting spirit of "the weaker sex".

When we got enough material to reach critical mass, we started assembling this initial volume. If the concept succeeds (naked girls and guns - c'mon!), it's a fair bet we'll be back for more!

DANGEROUS CURVES

Volume One

Book design by Grassy Knoll Studios.
Cover artwork by Dave Dunstan

Published by
SQP Inc.
PO Box 248 - Columbus, NJ 08022

Sal Quartuccio & Bob Keenan - Publishers

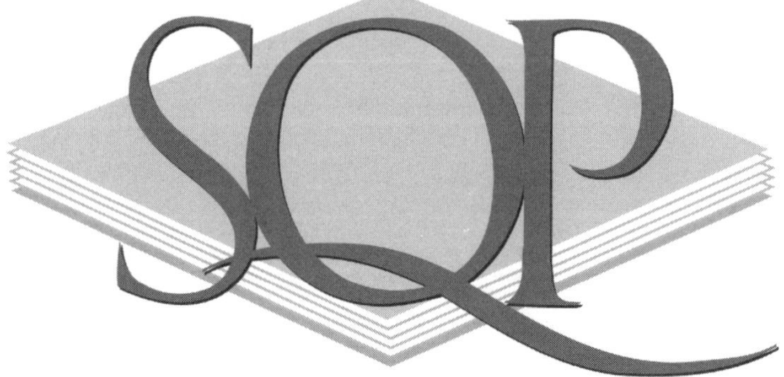

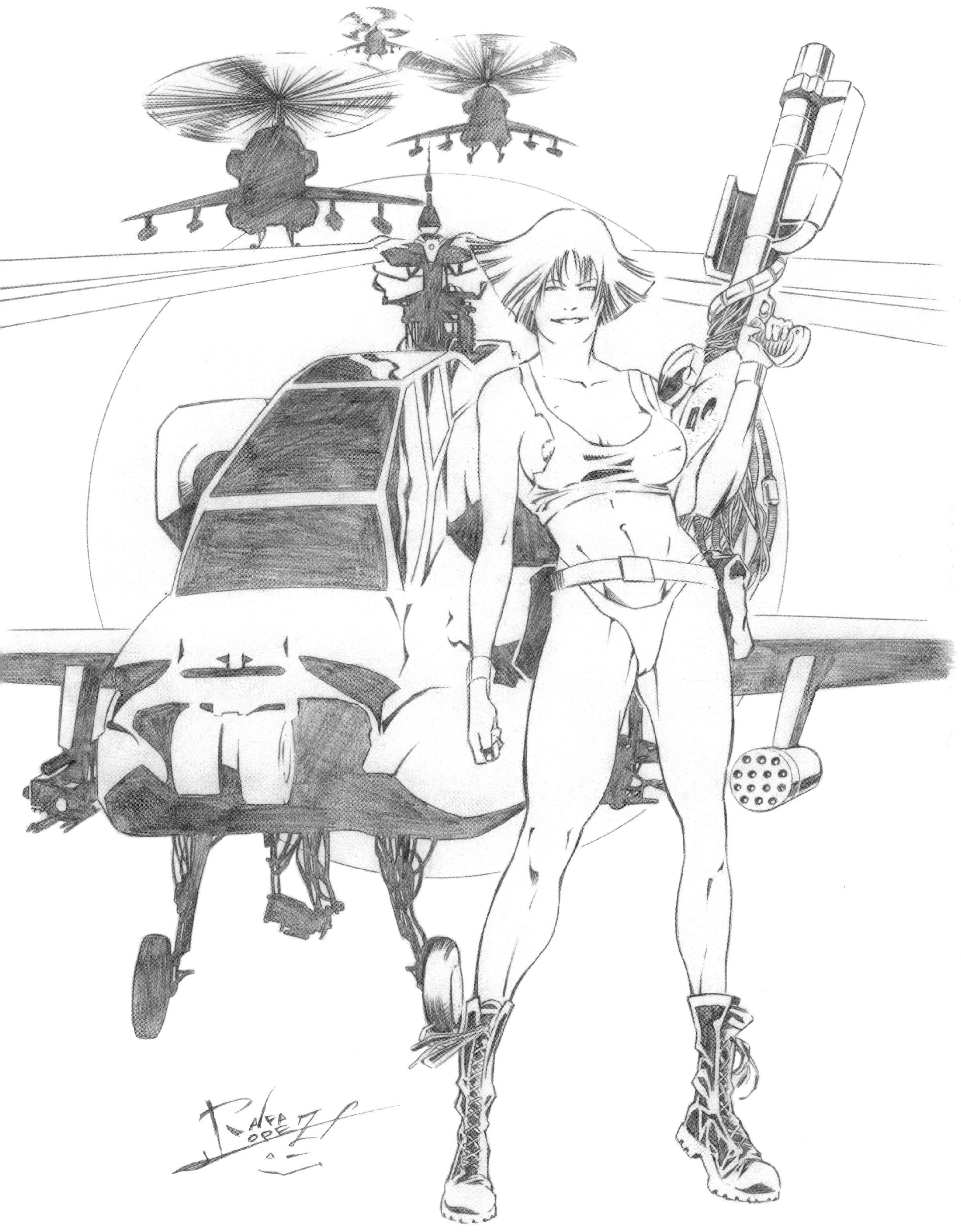

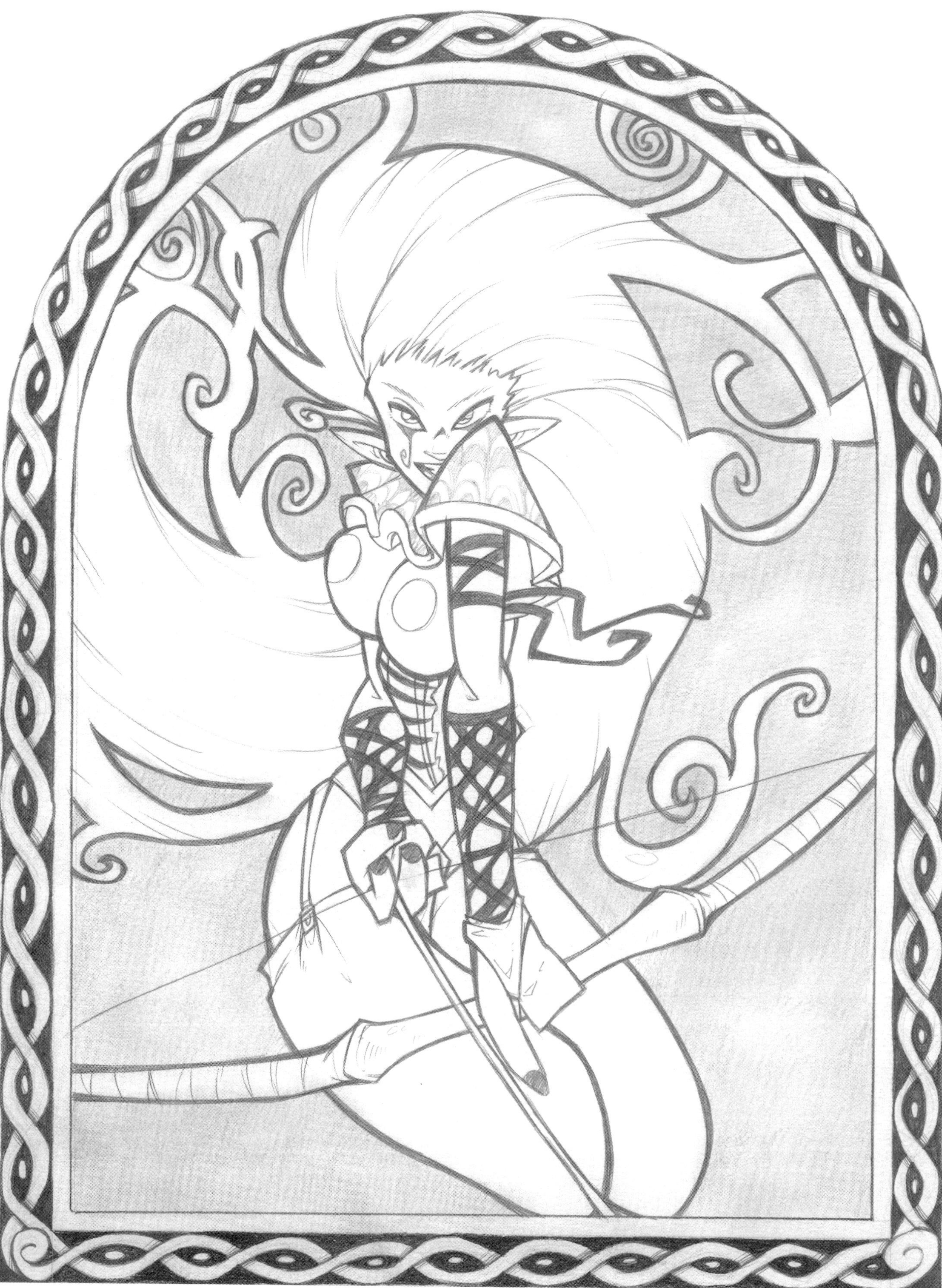

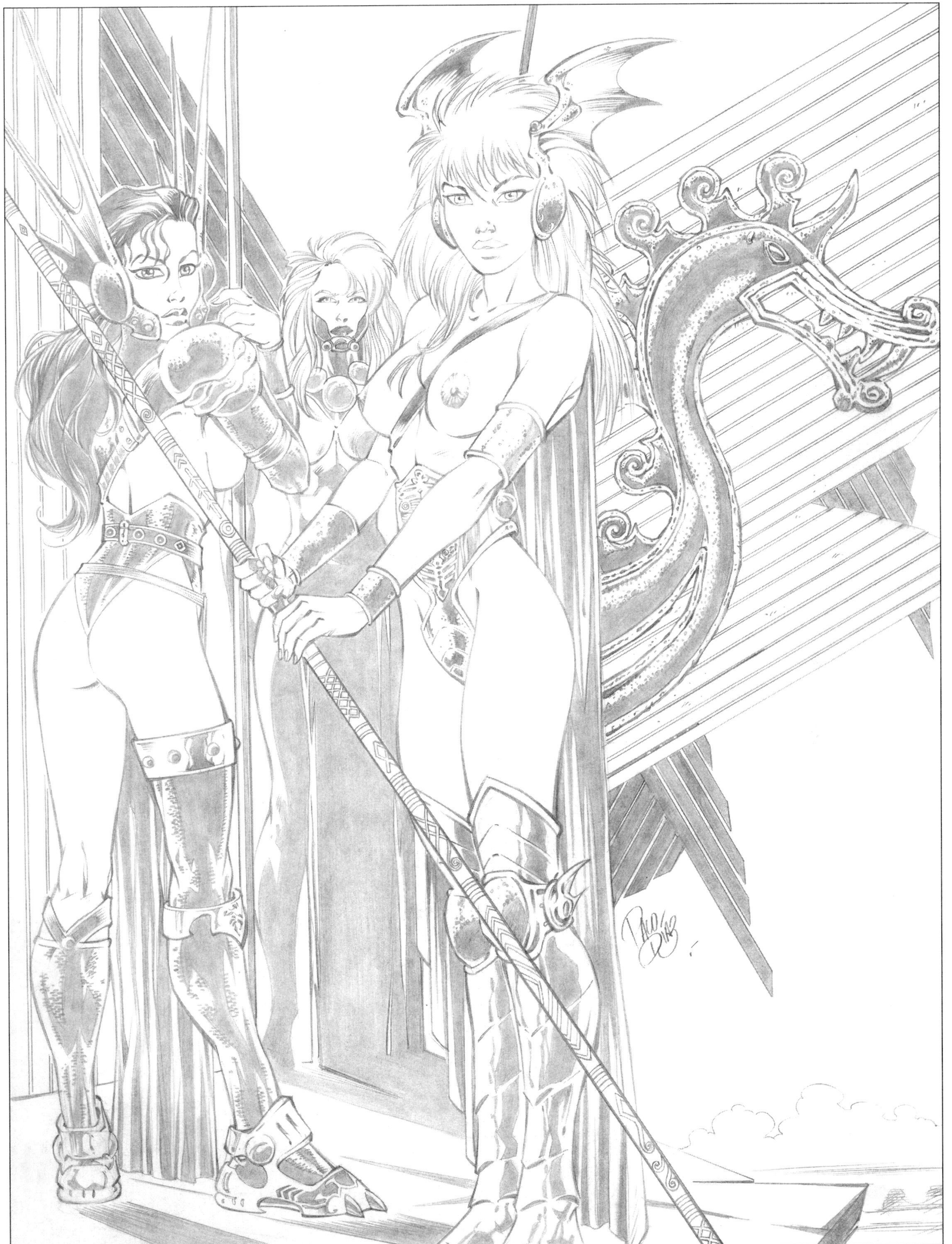

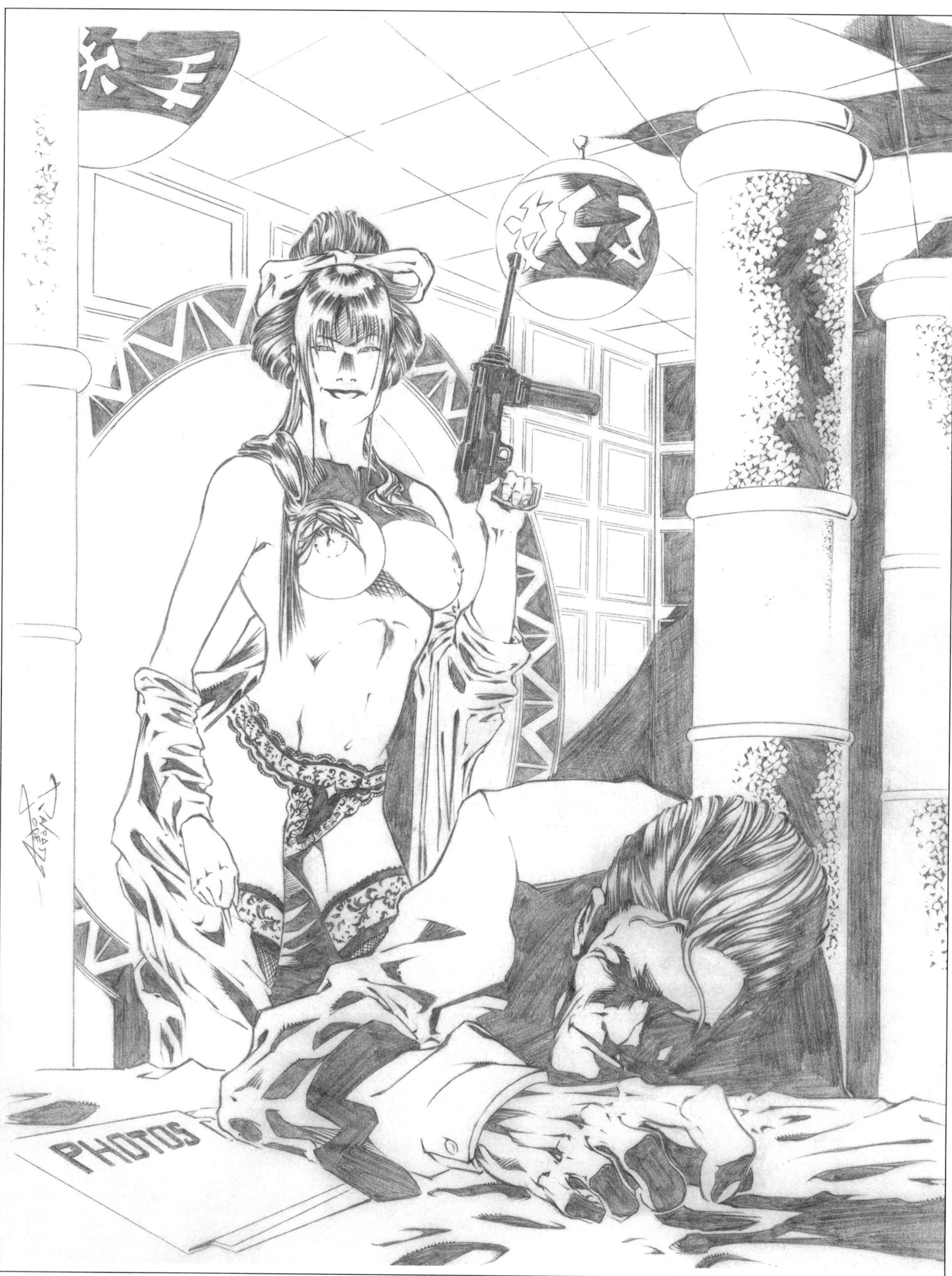
PHOTOS

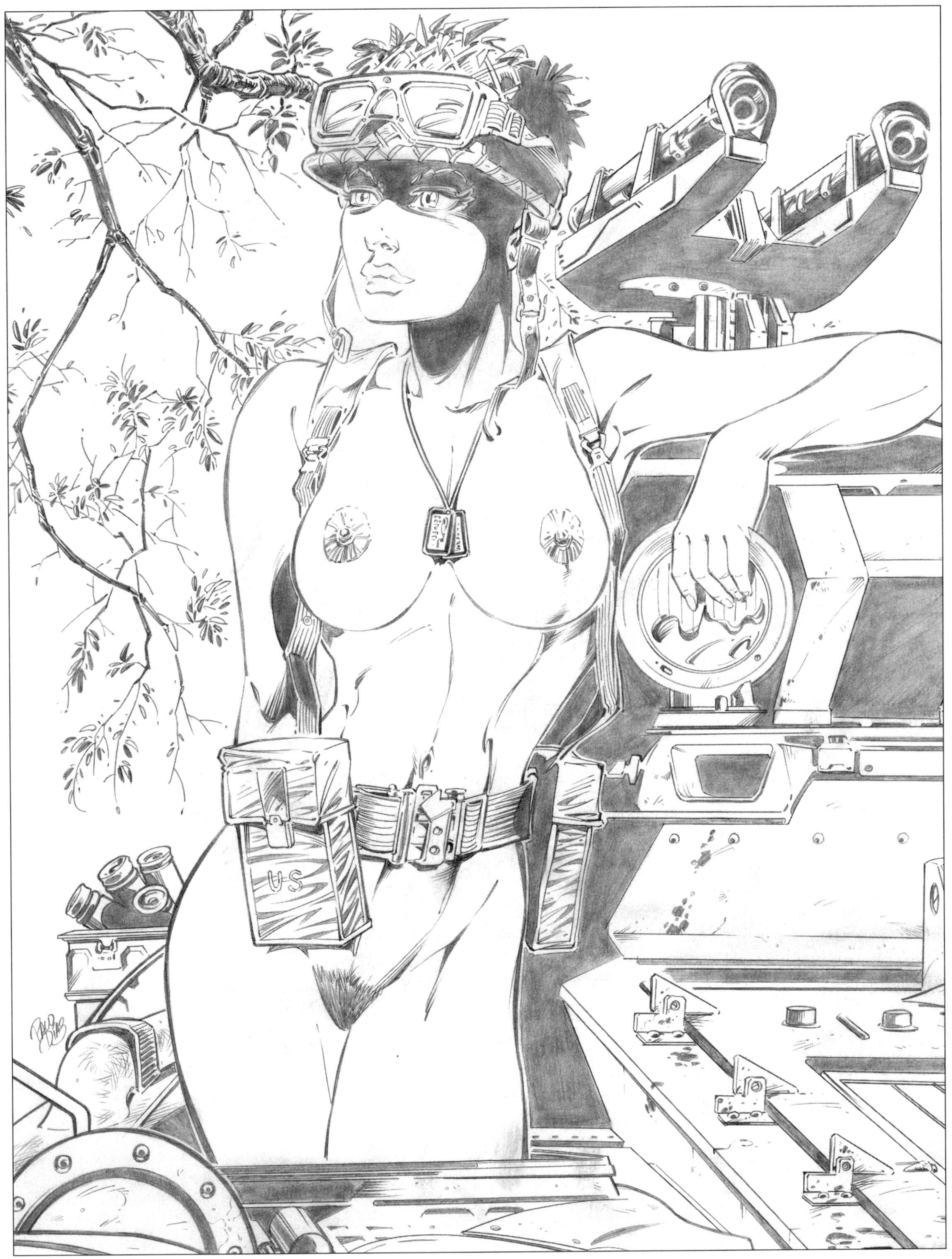
US

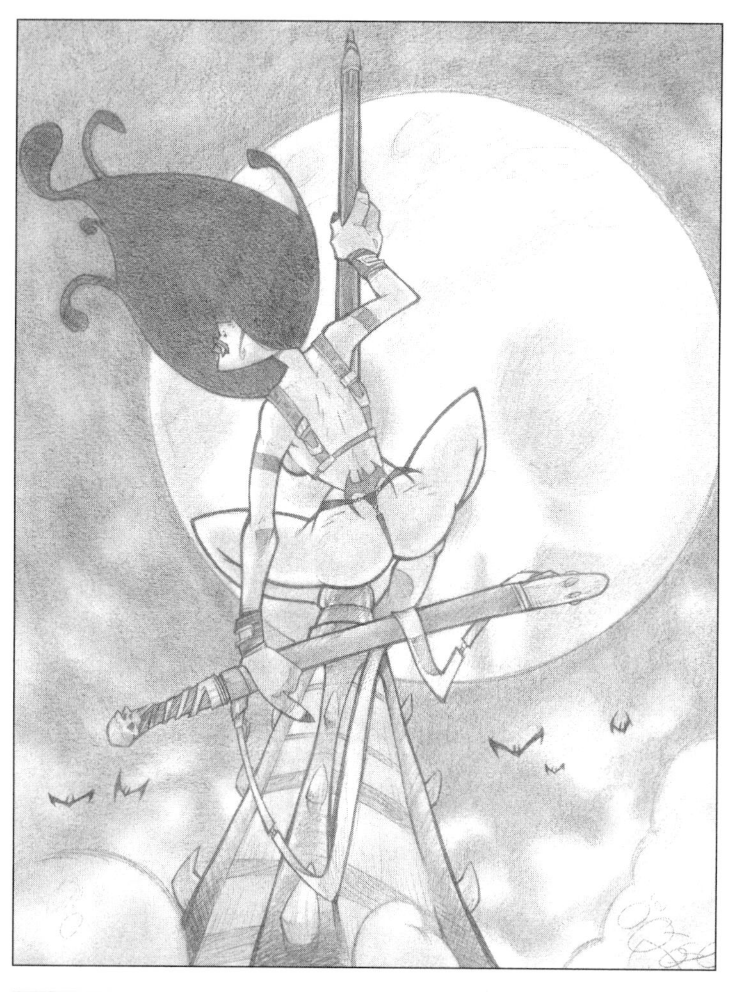
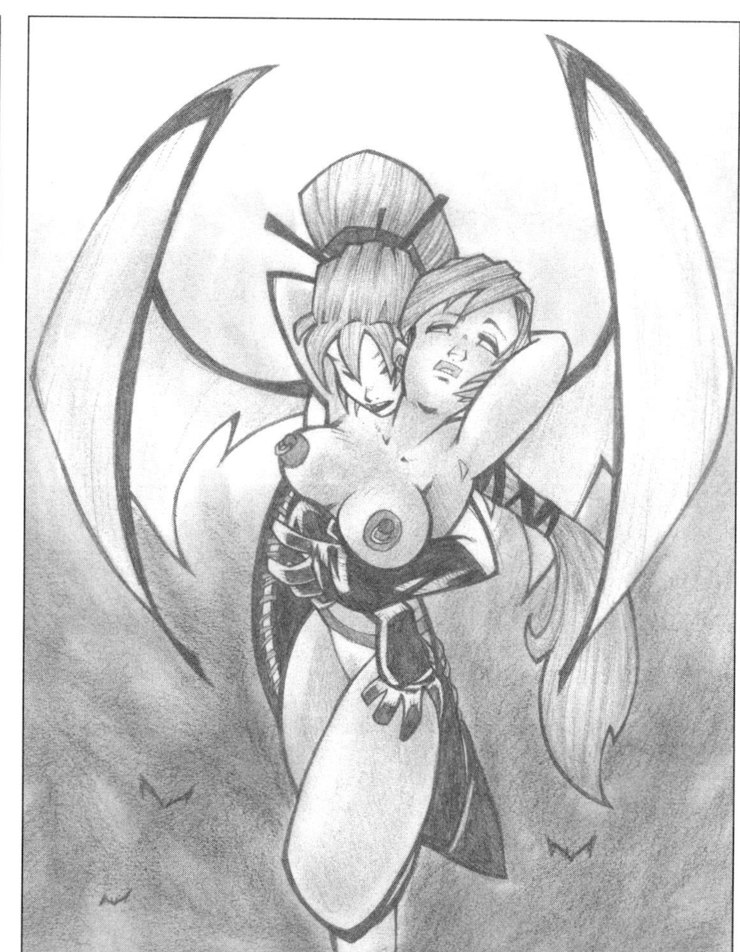
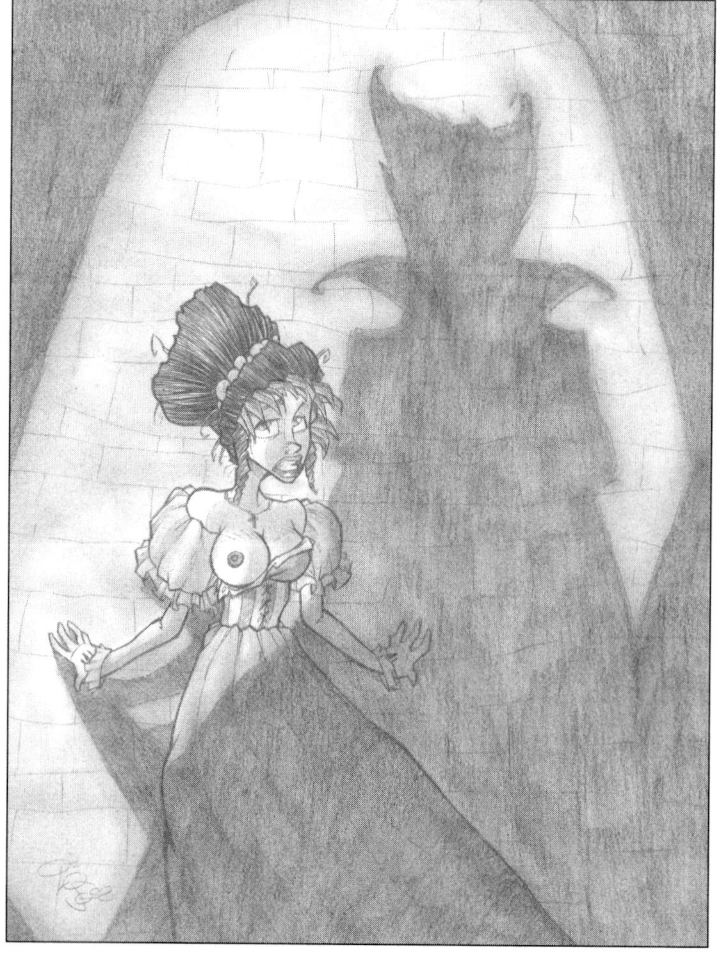
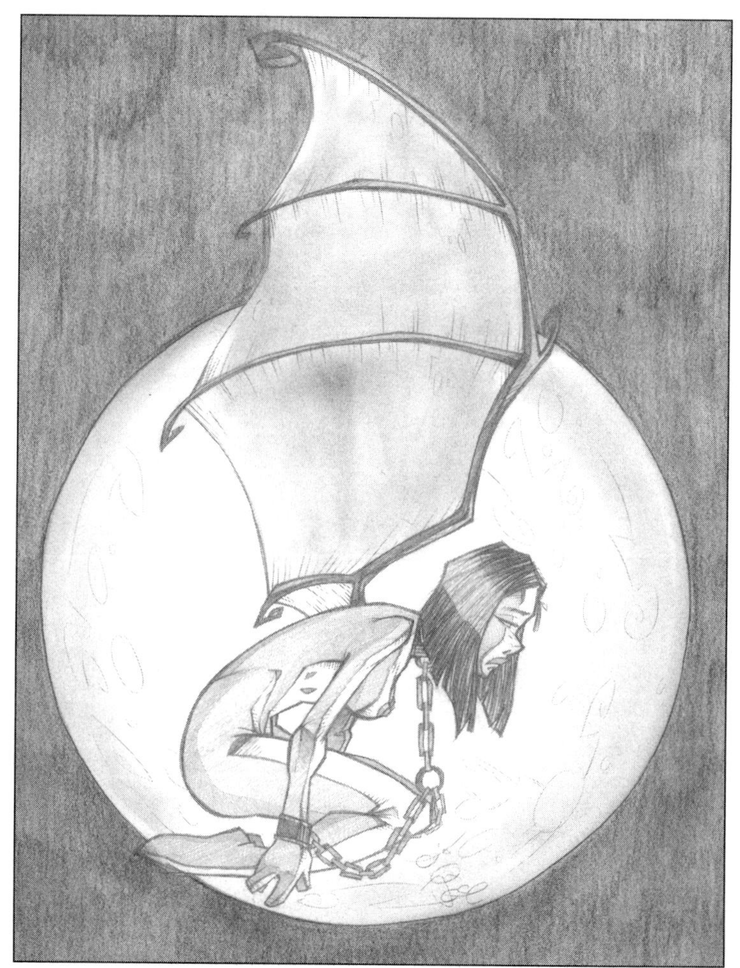

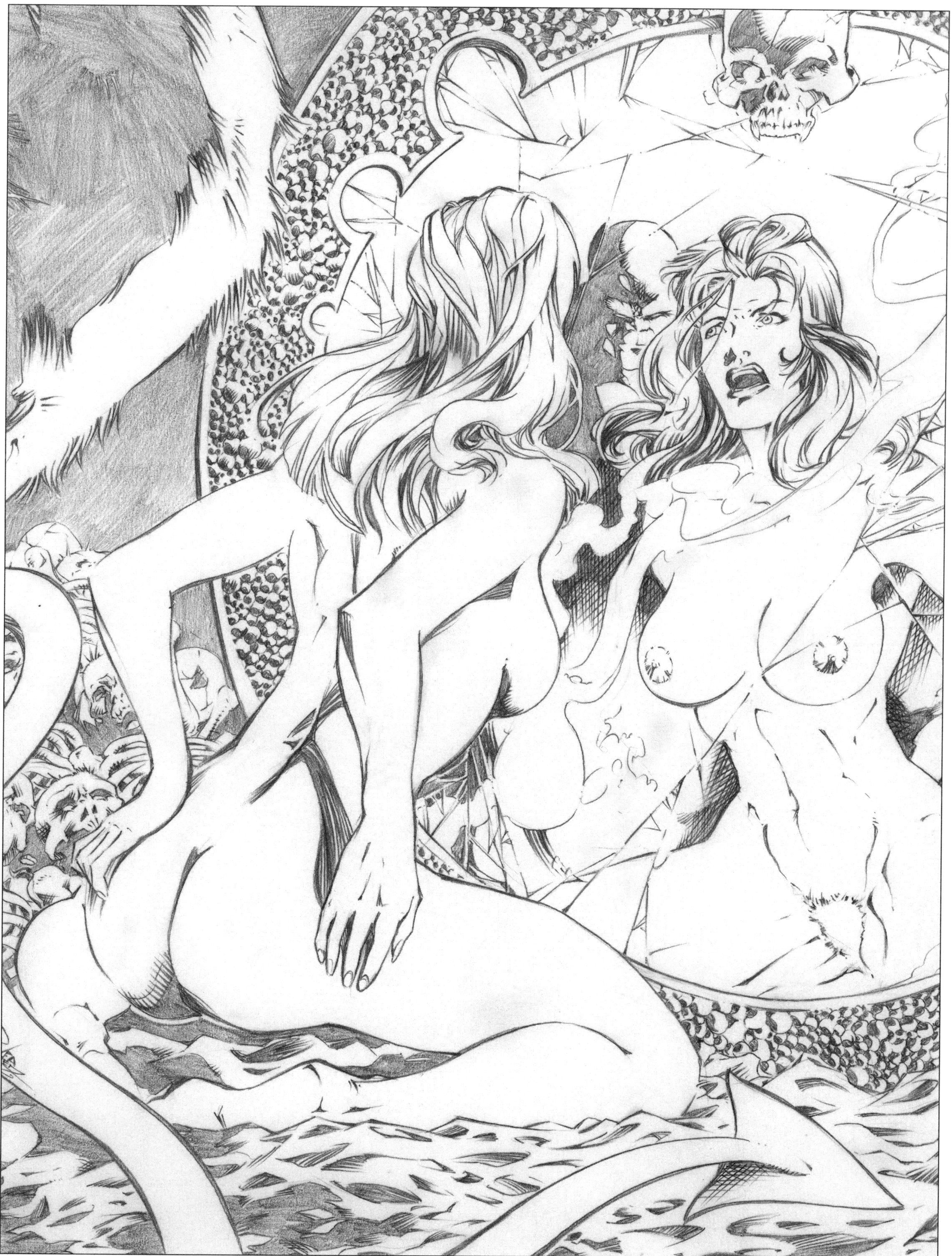

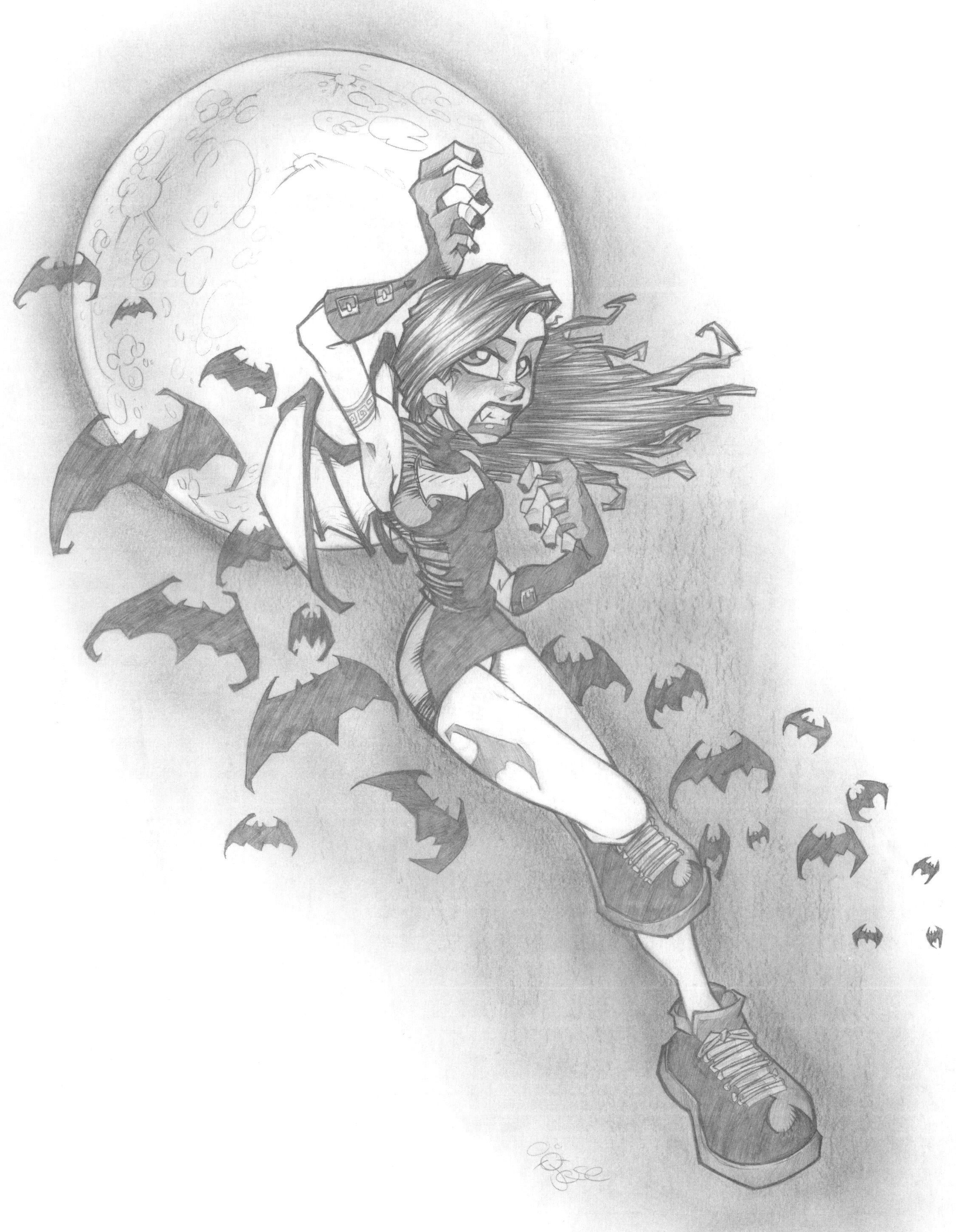

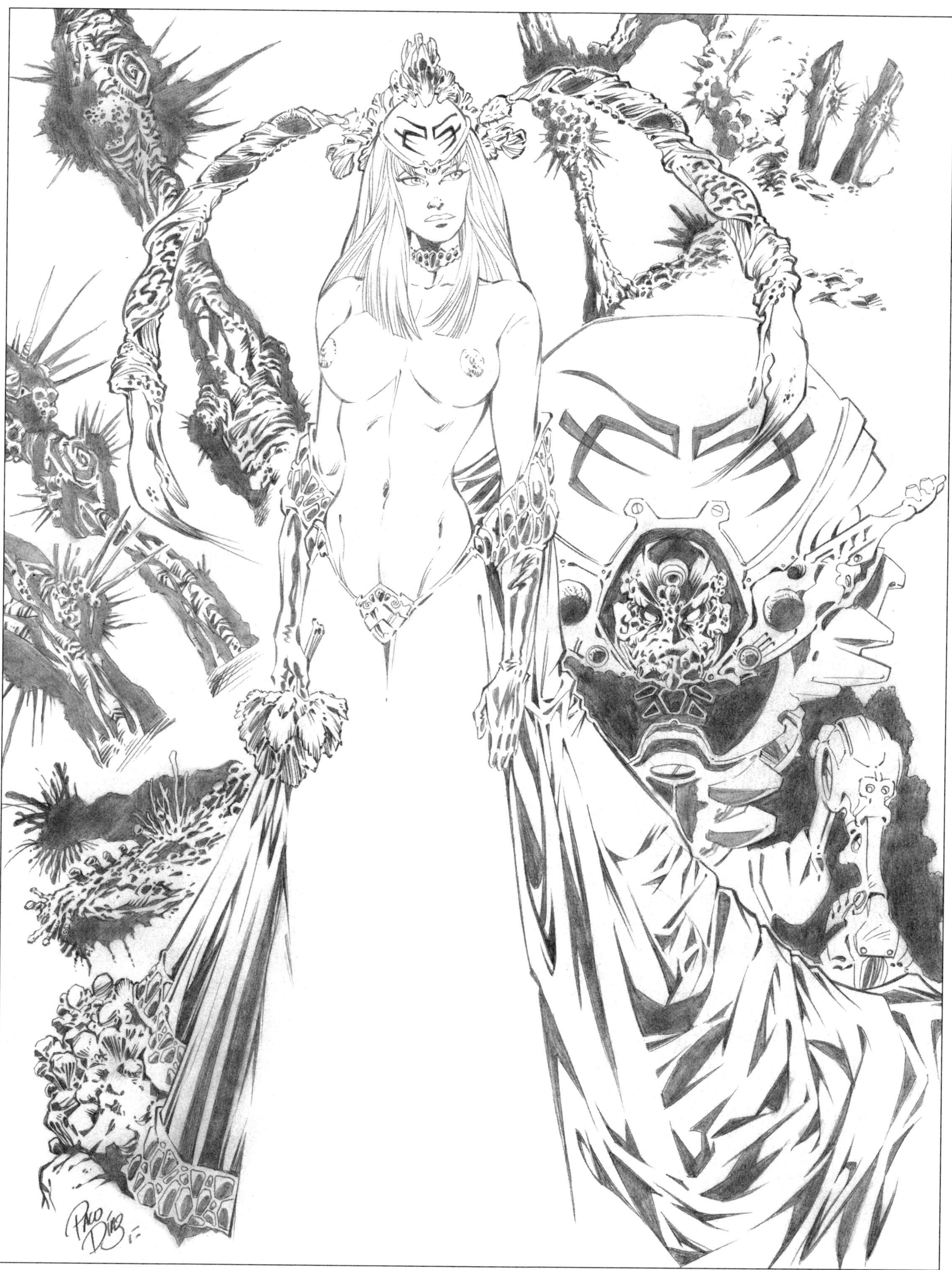
Paco Díaz

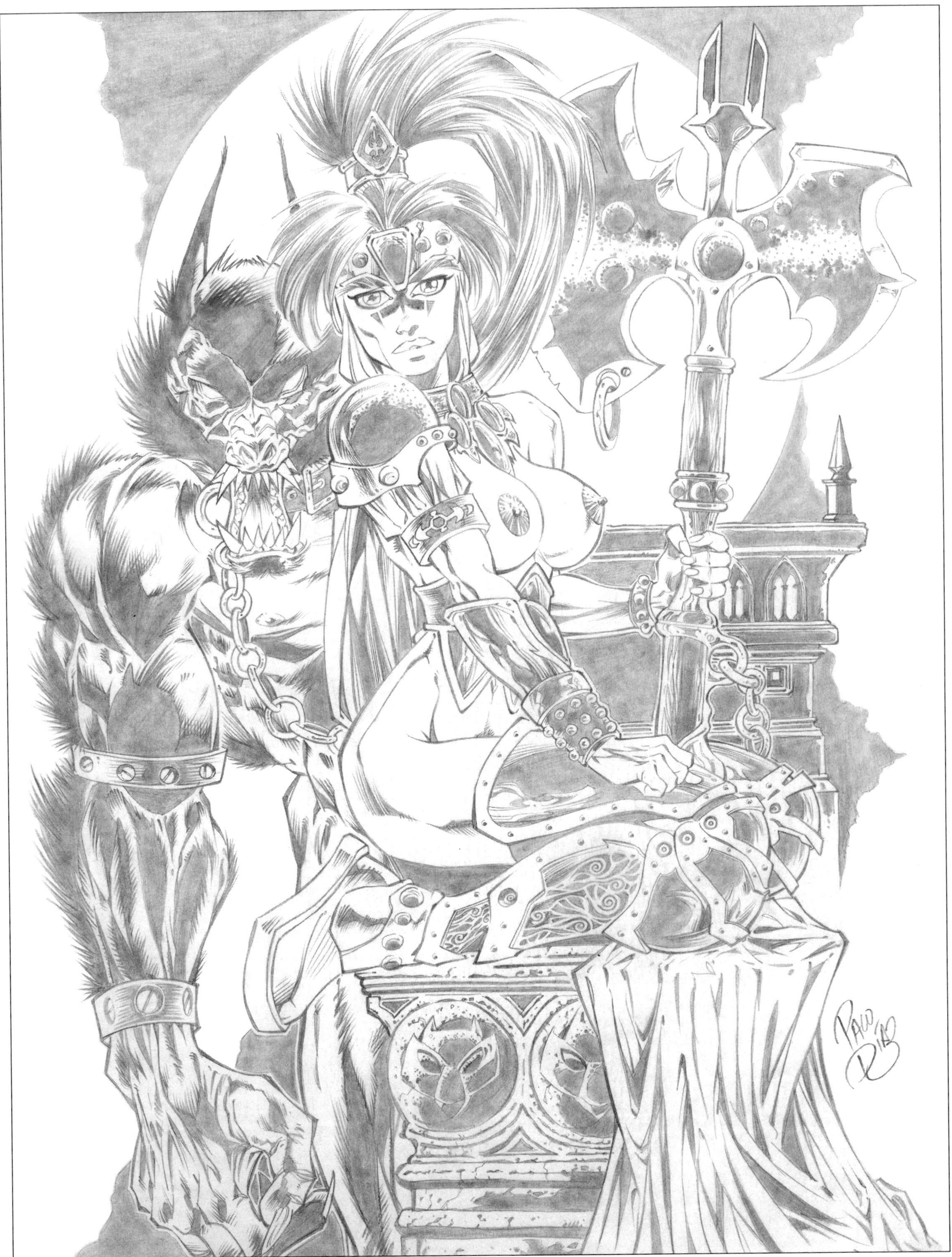

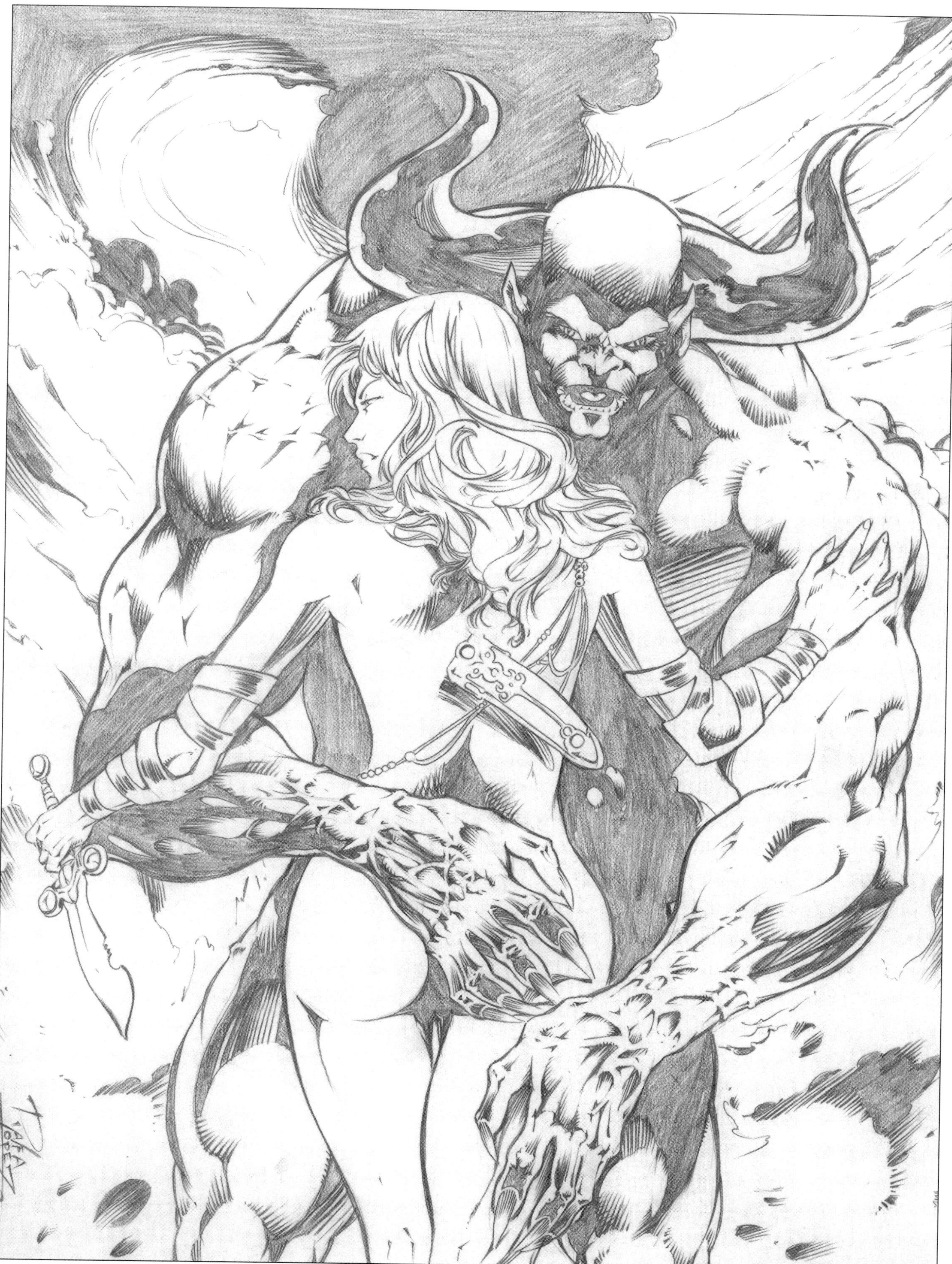

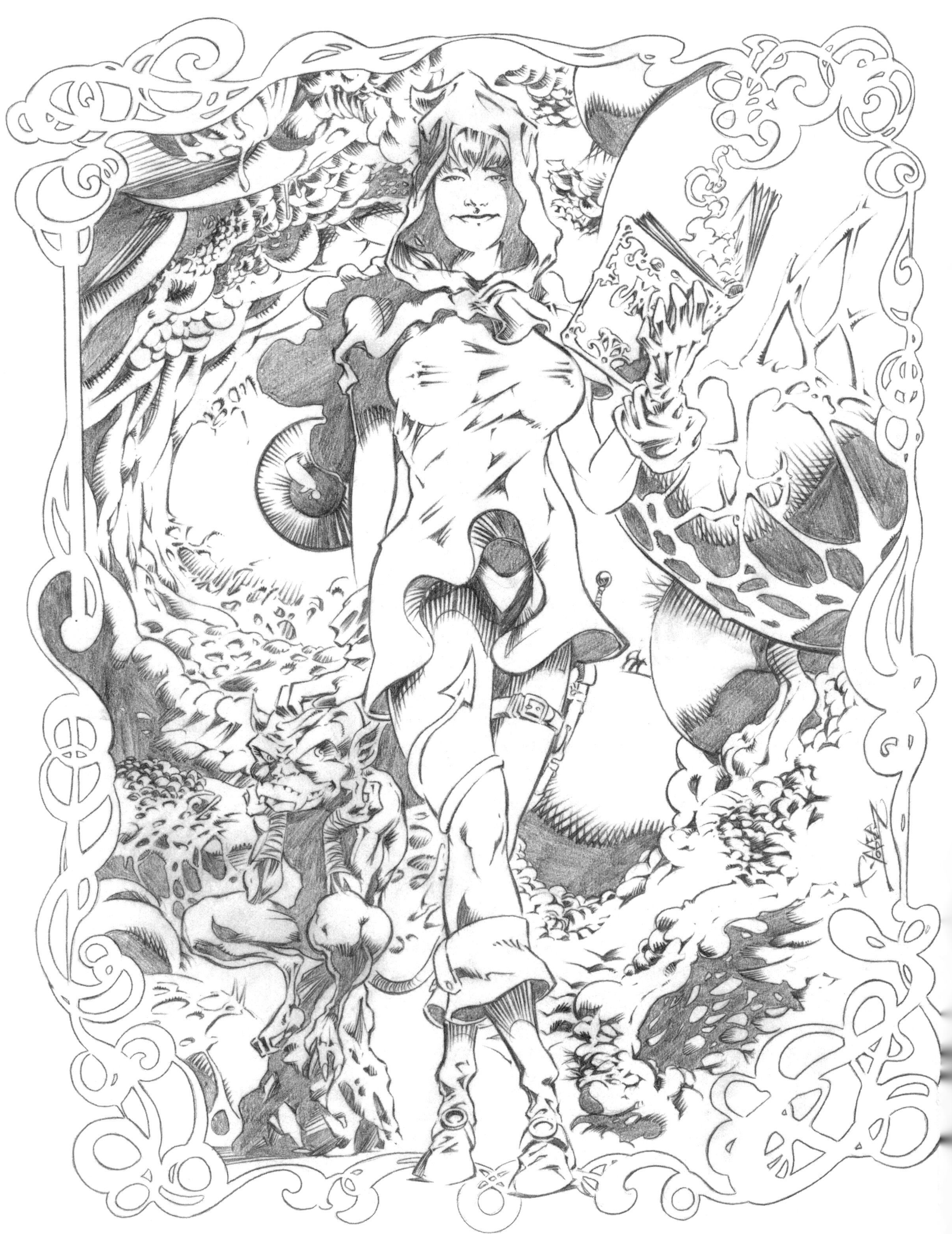

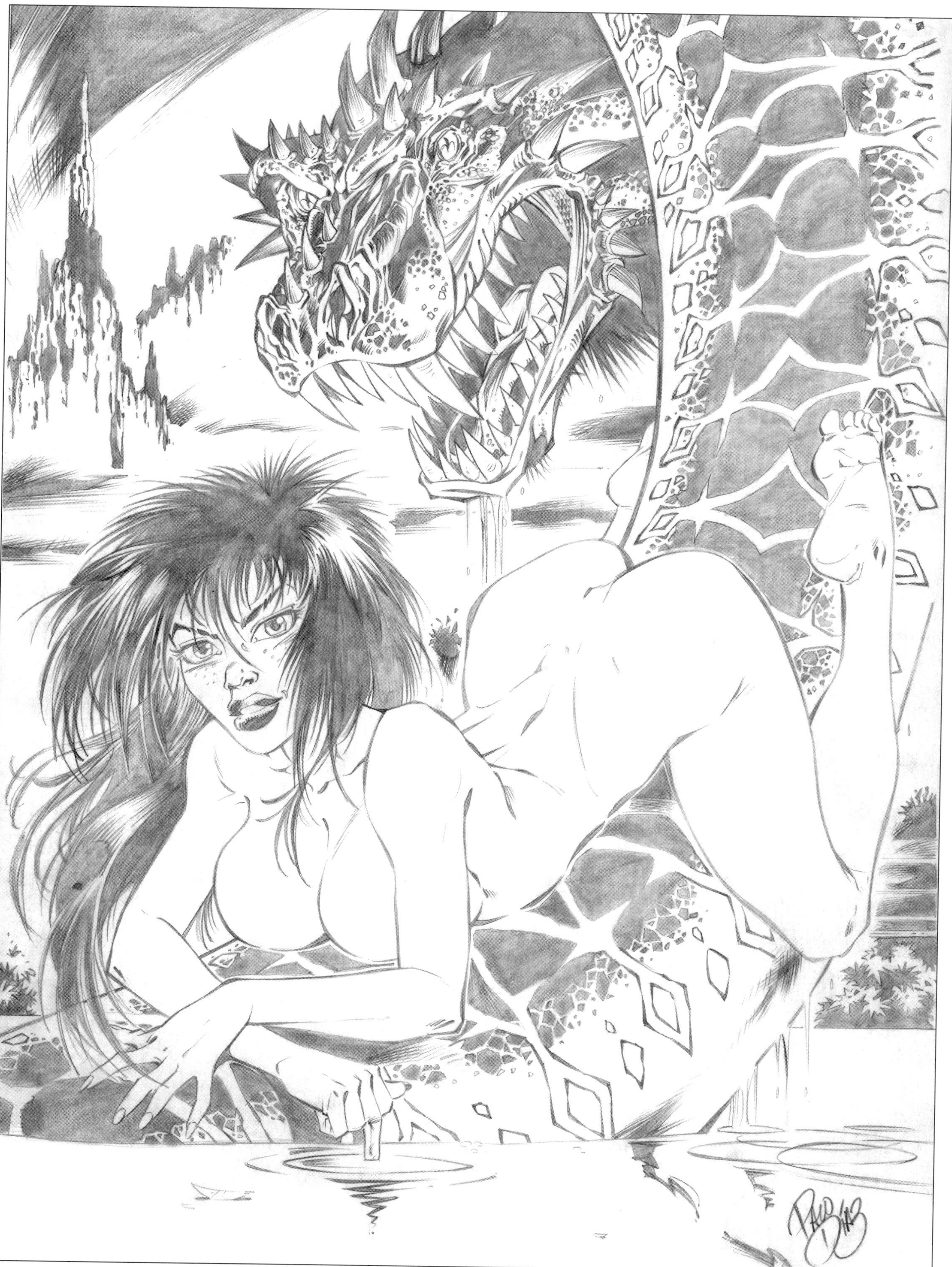

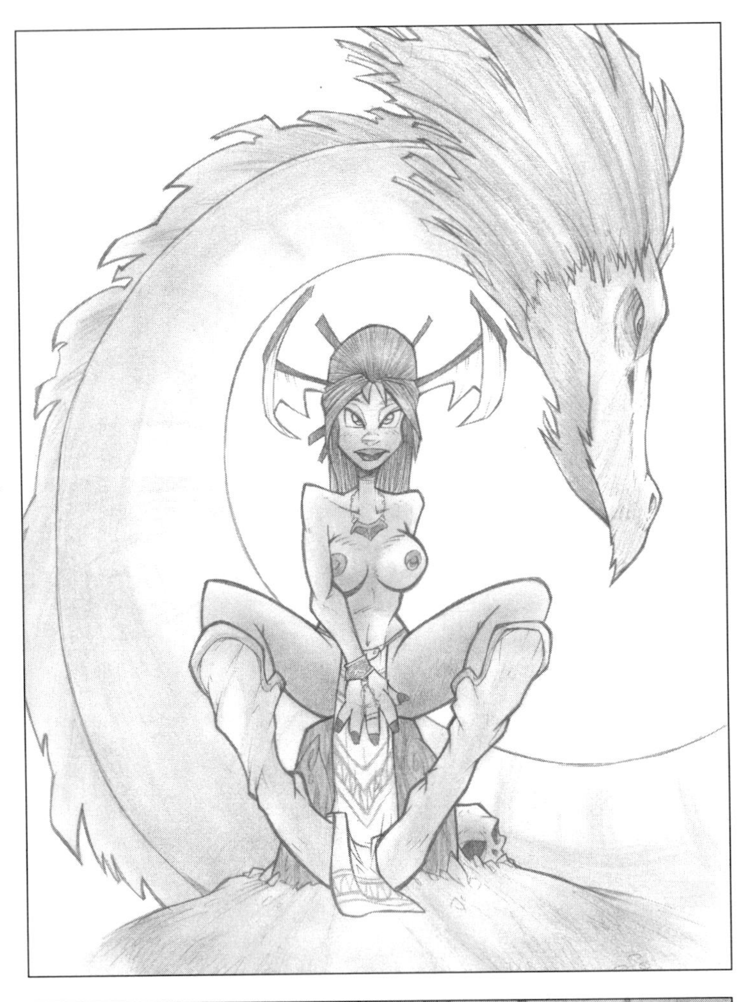
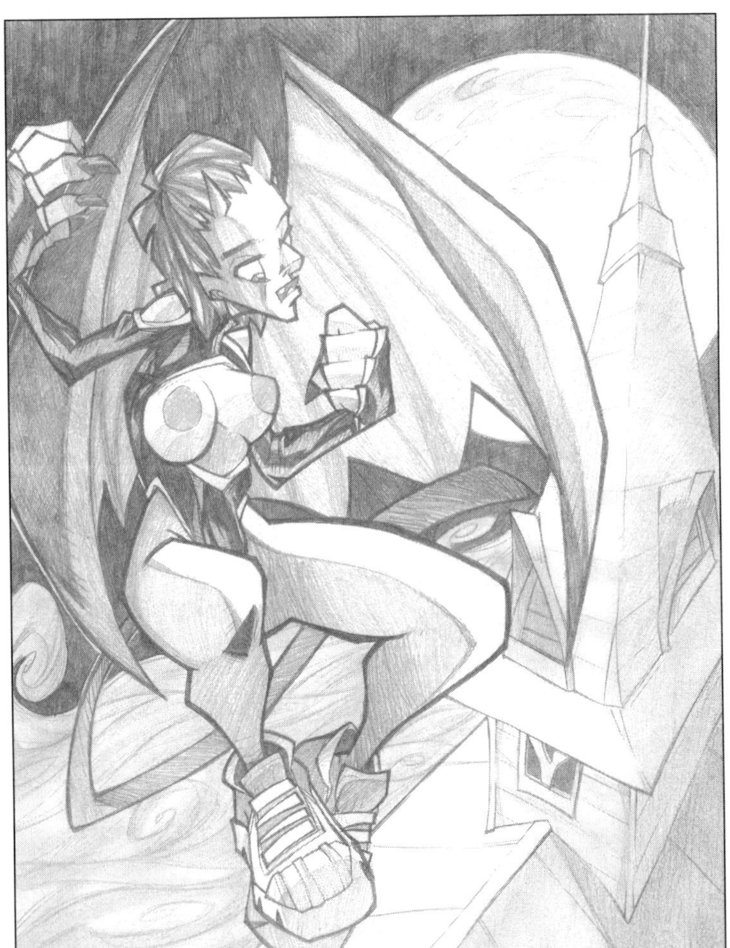
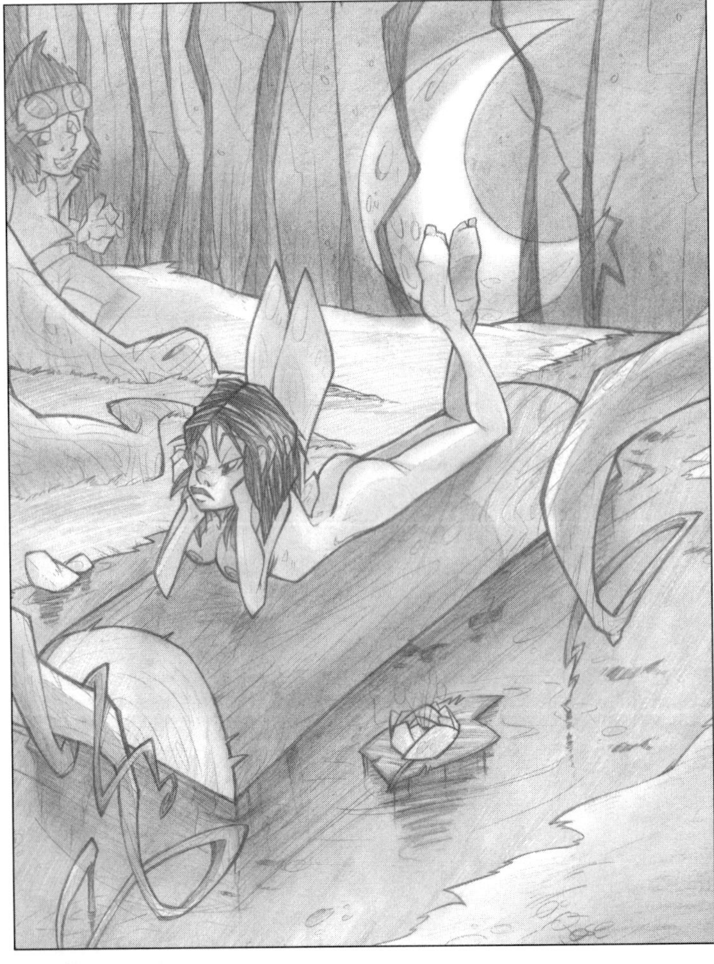
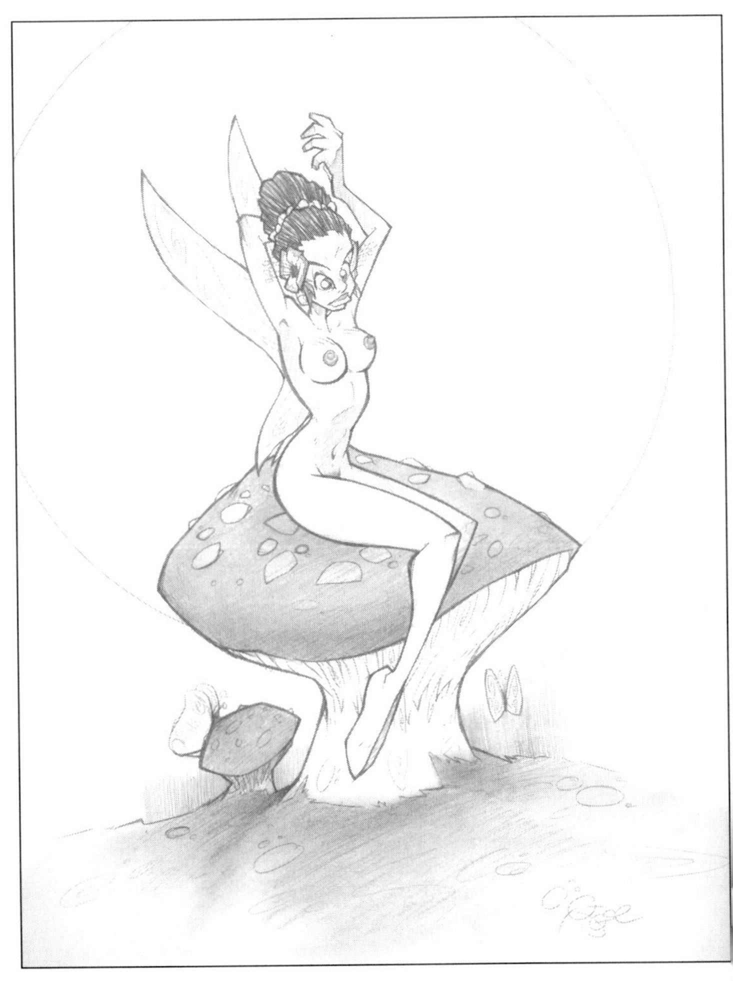

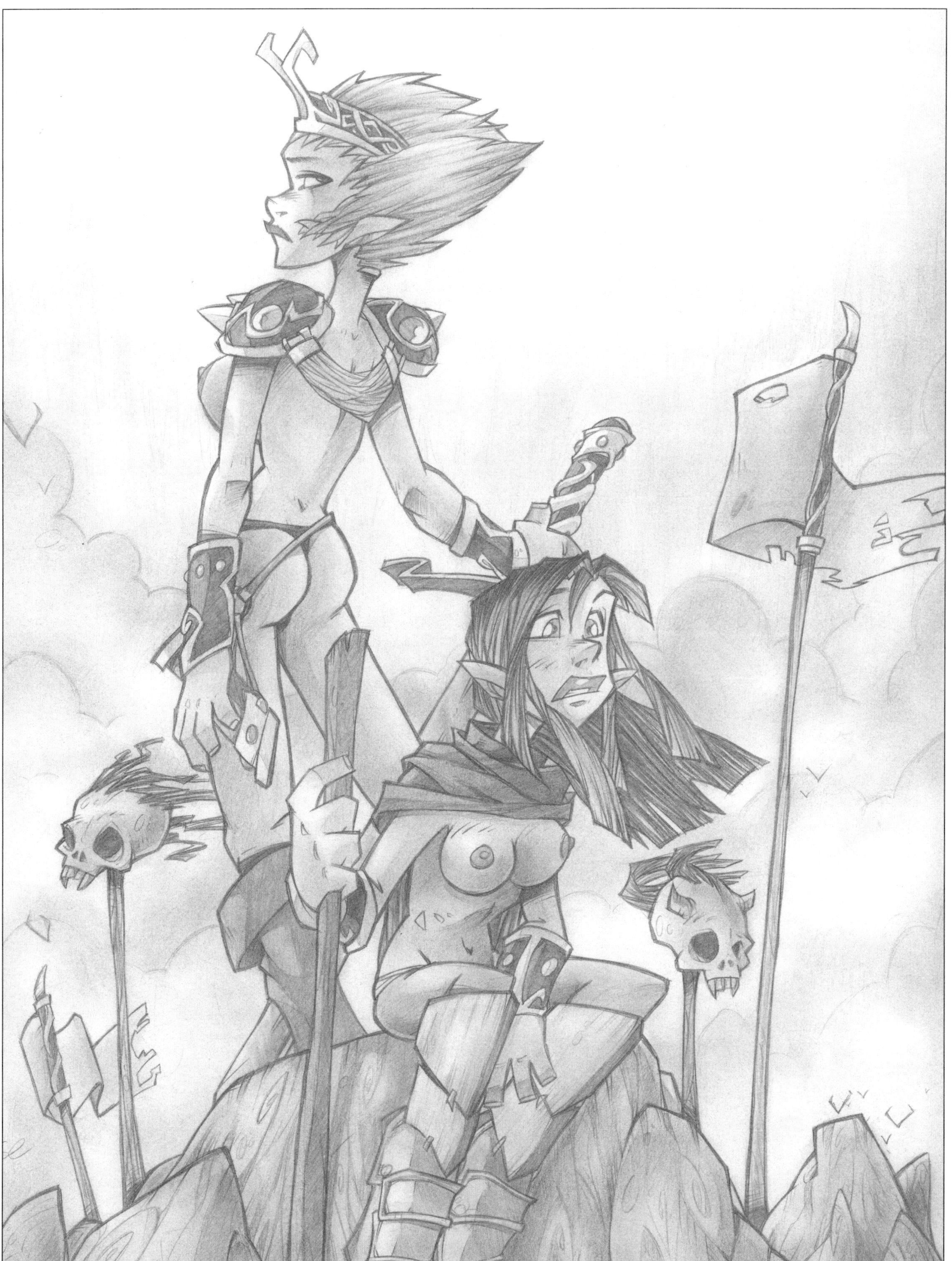

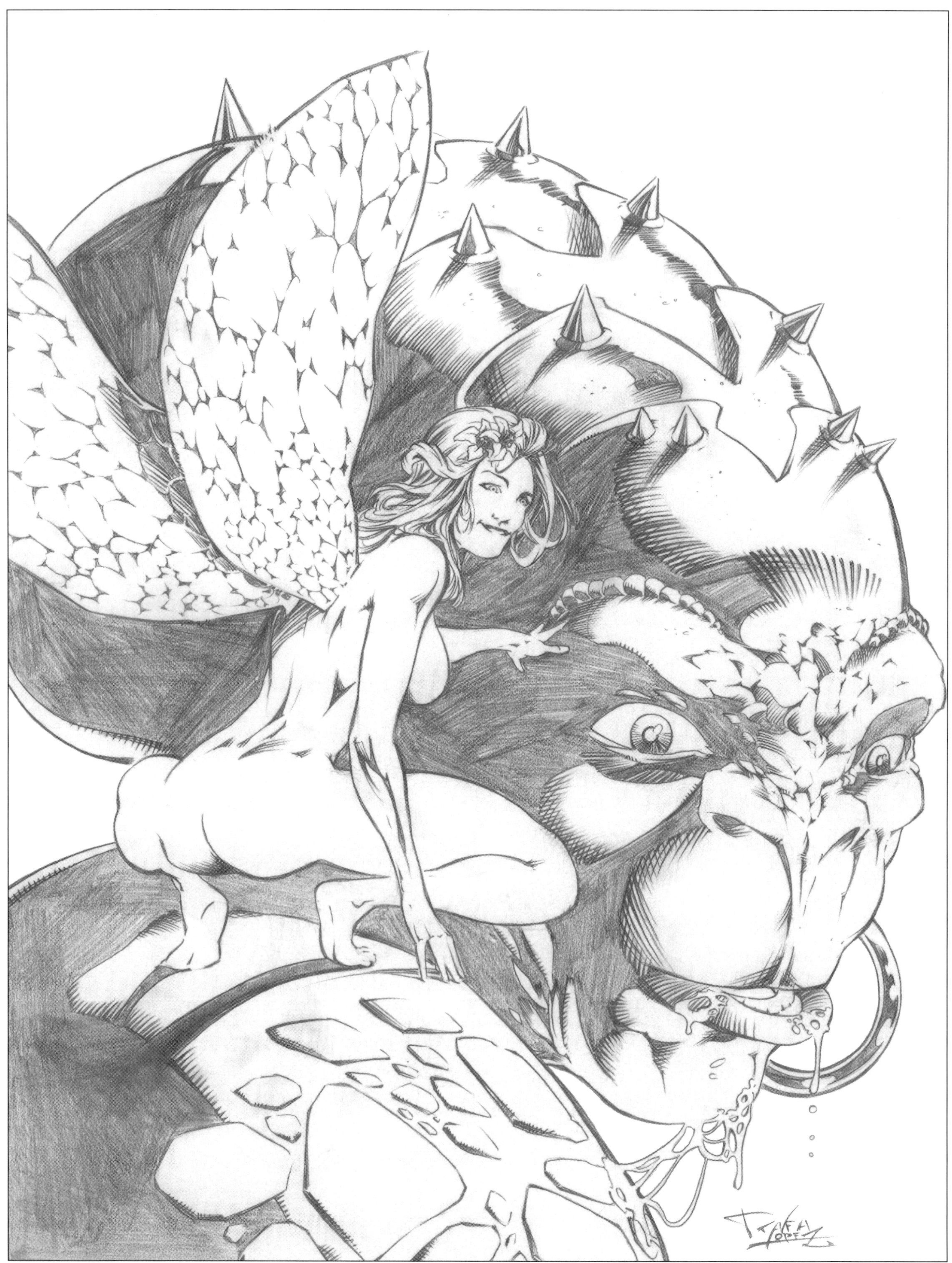

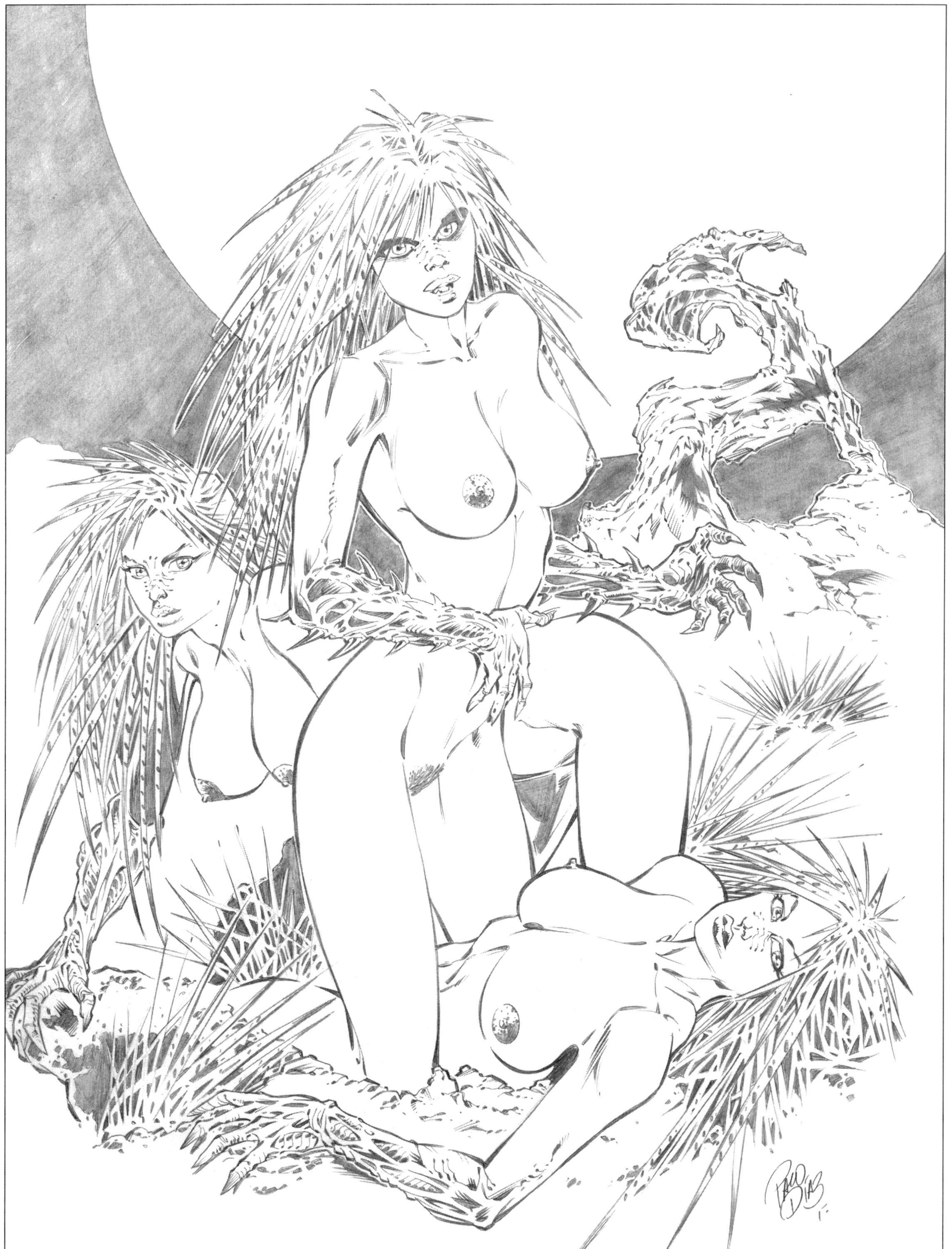

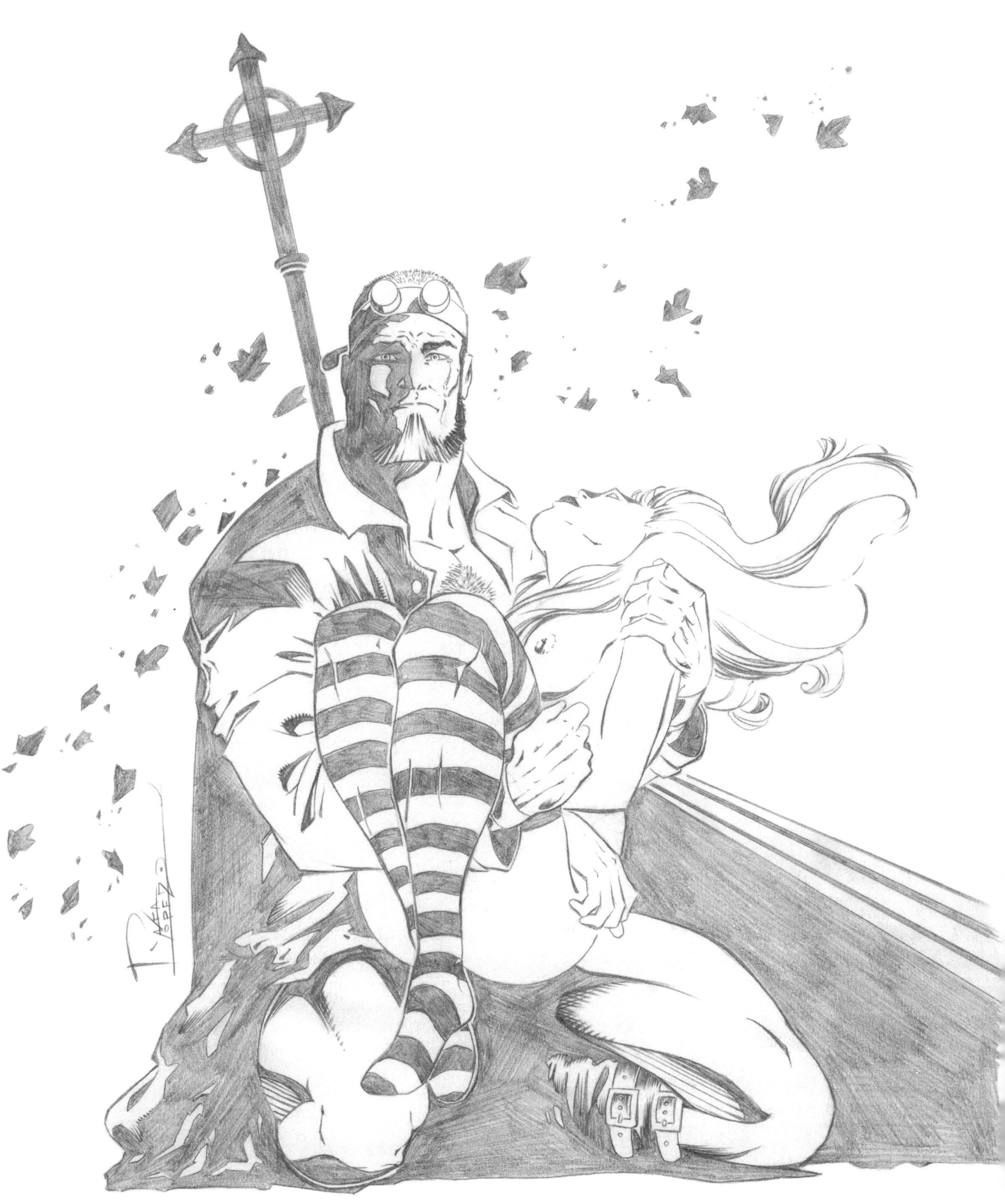

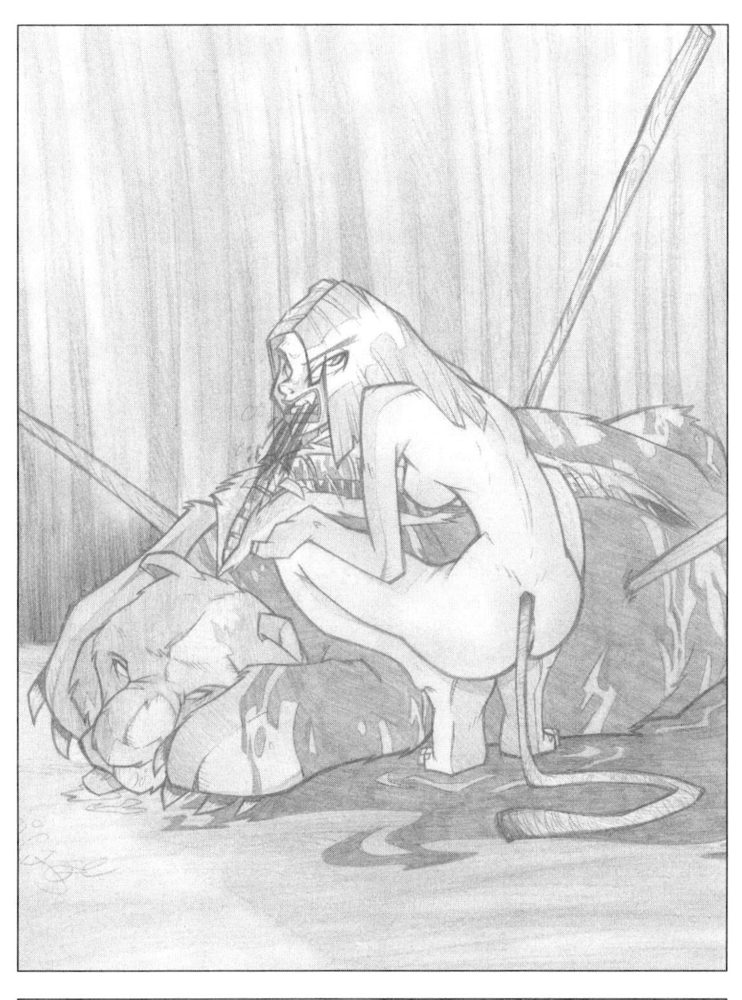
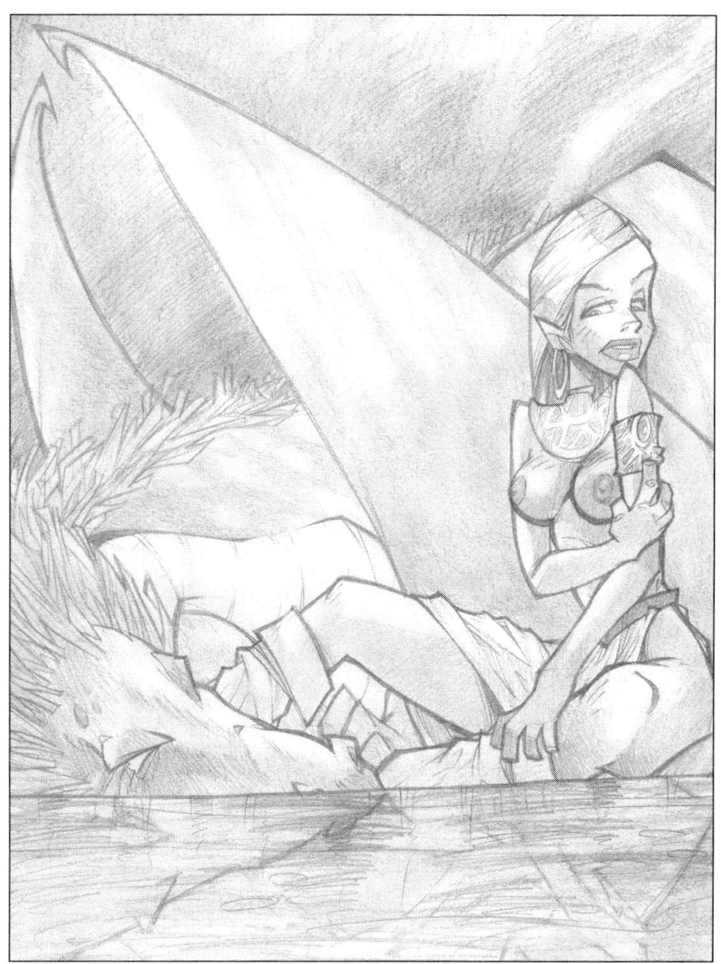
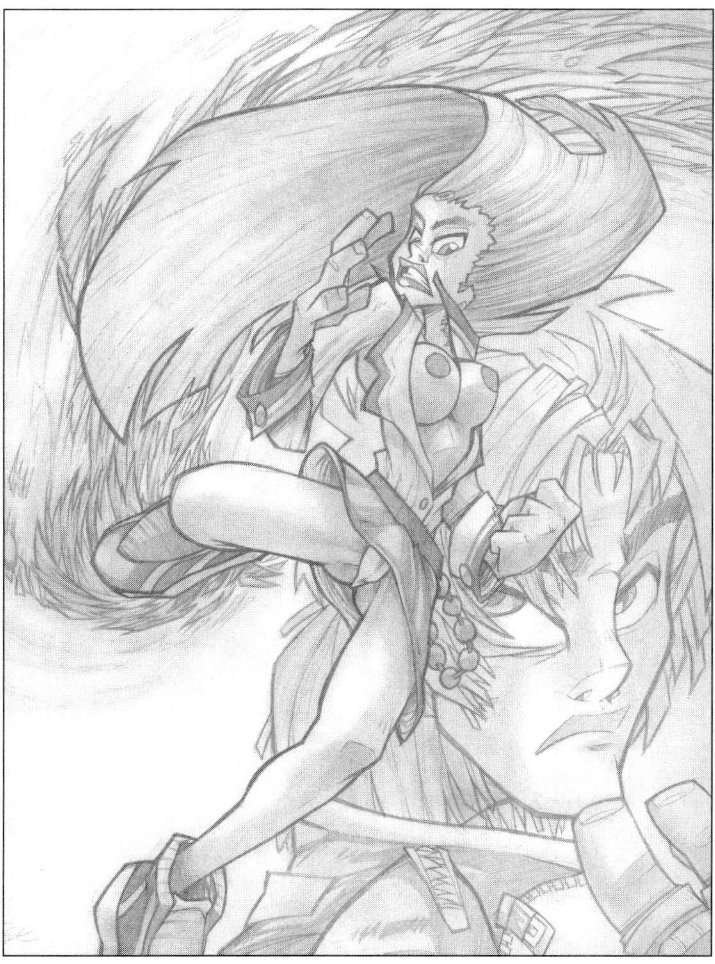
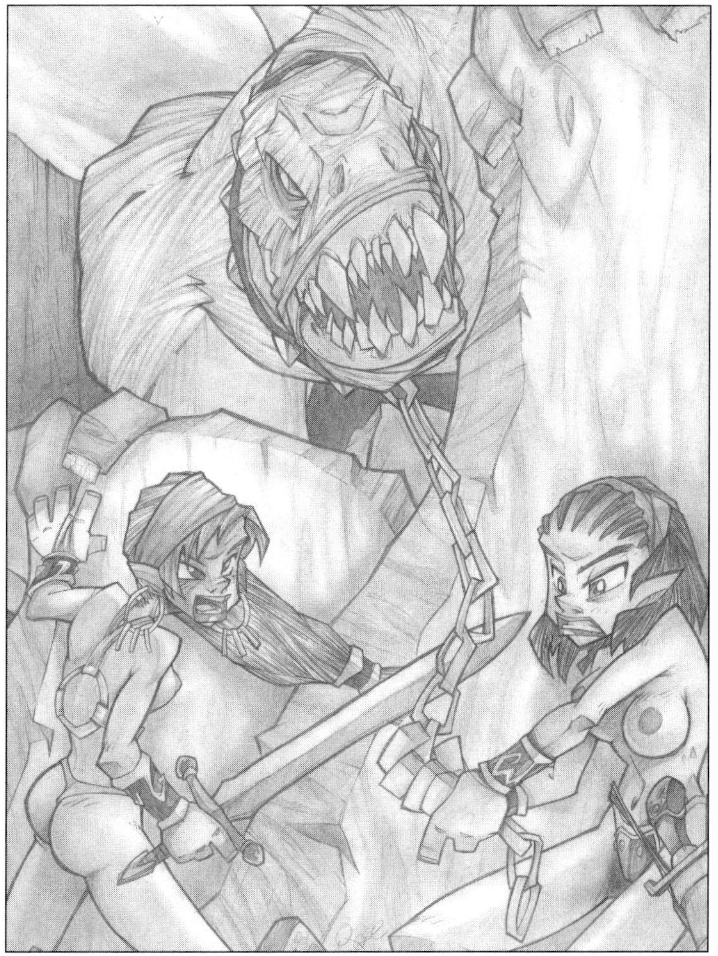

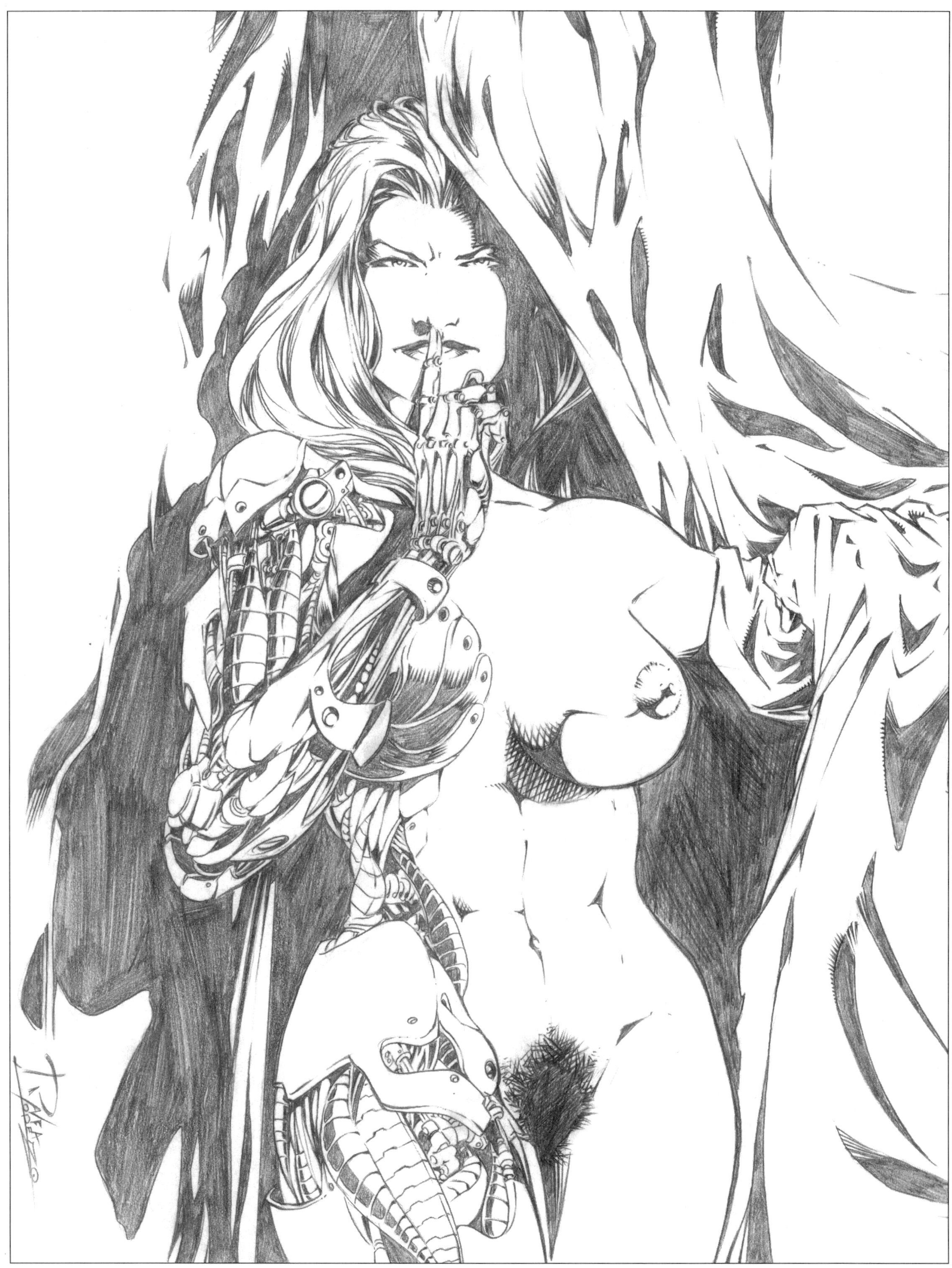

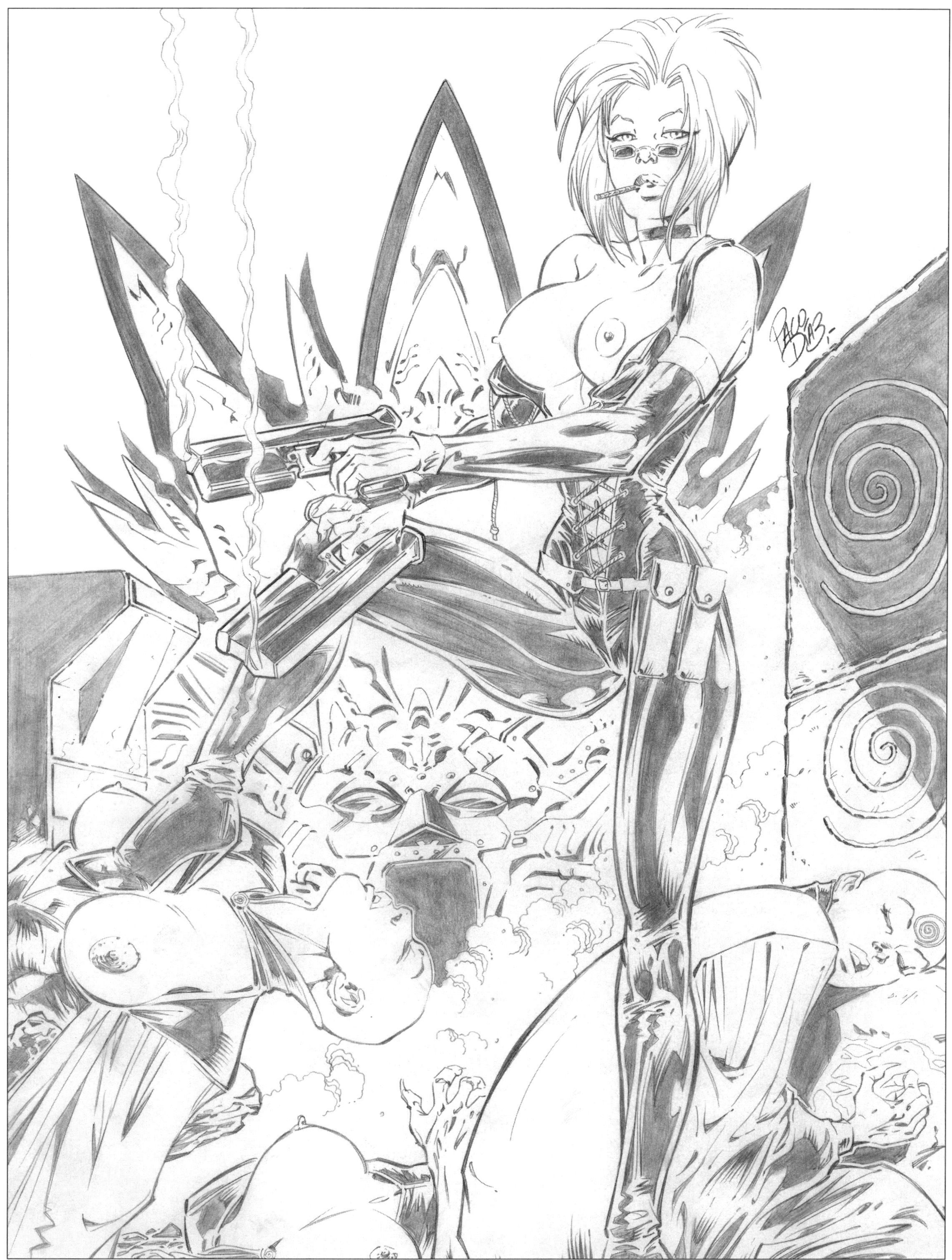

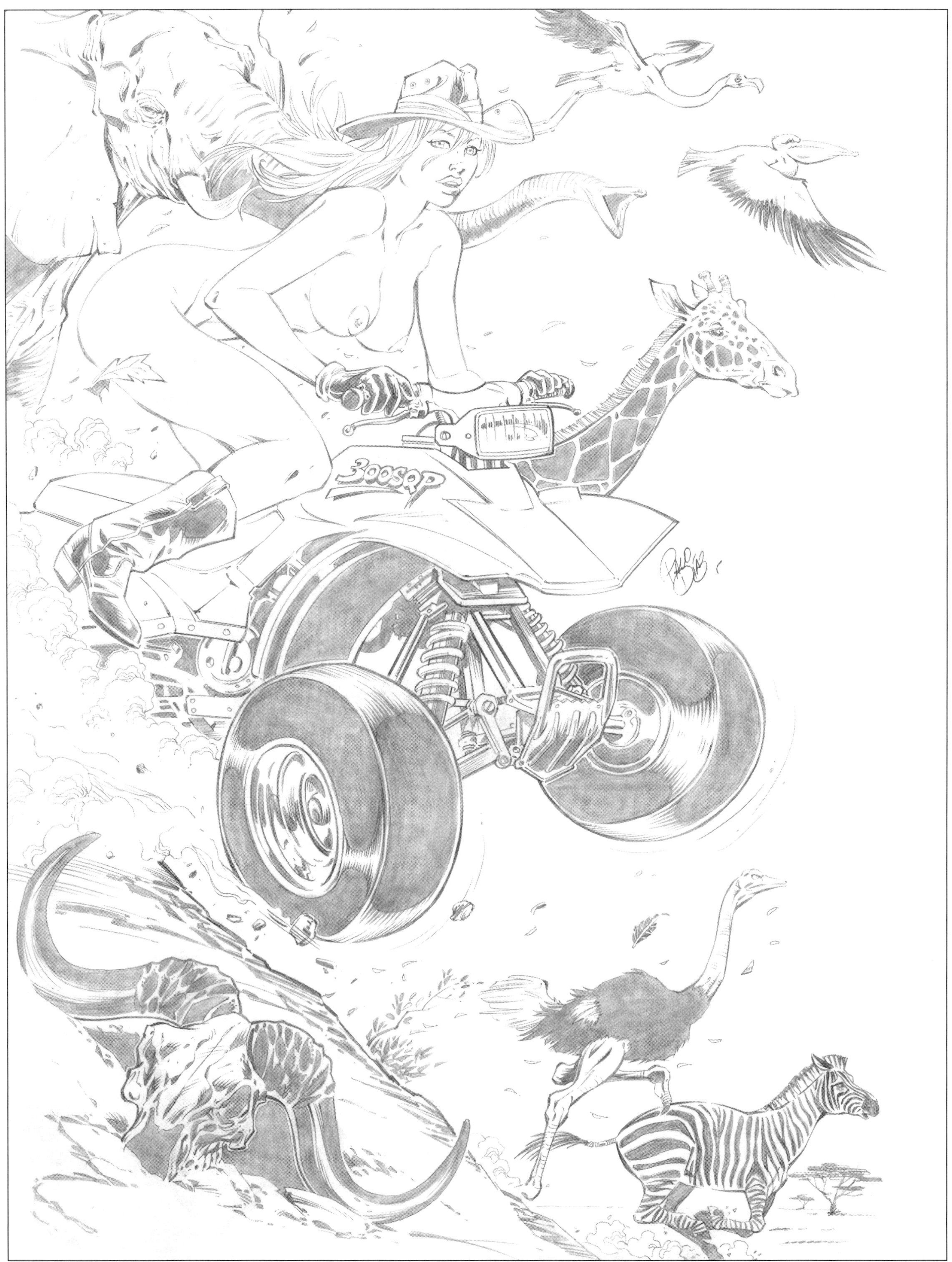
300SQP

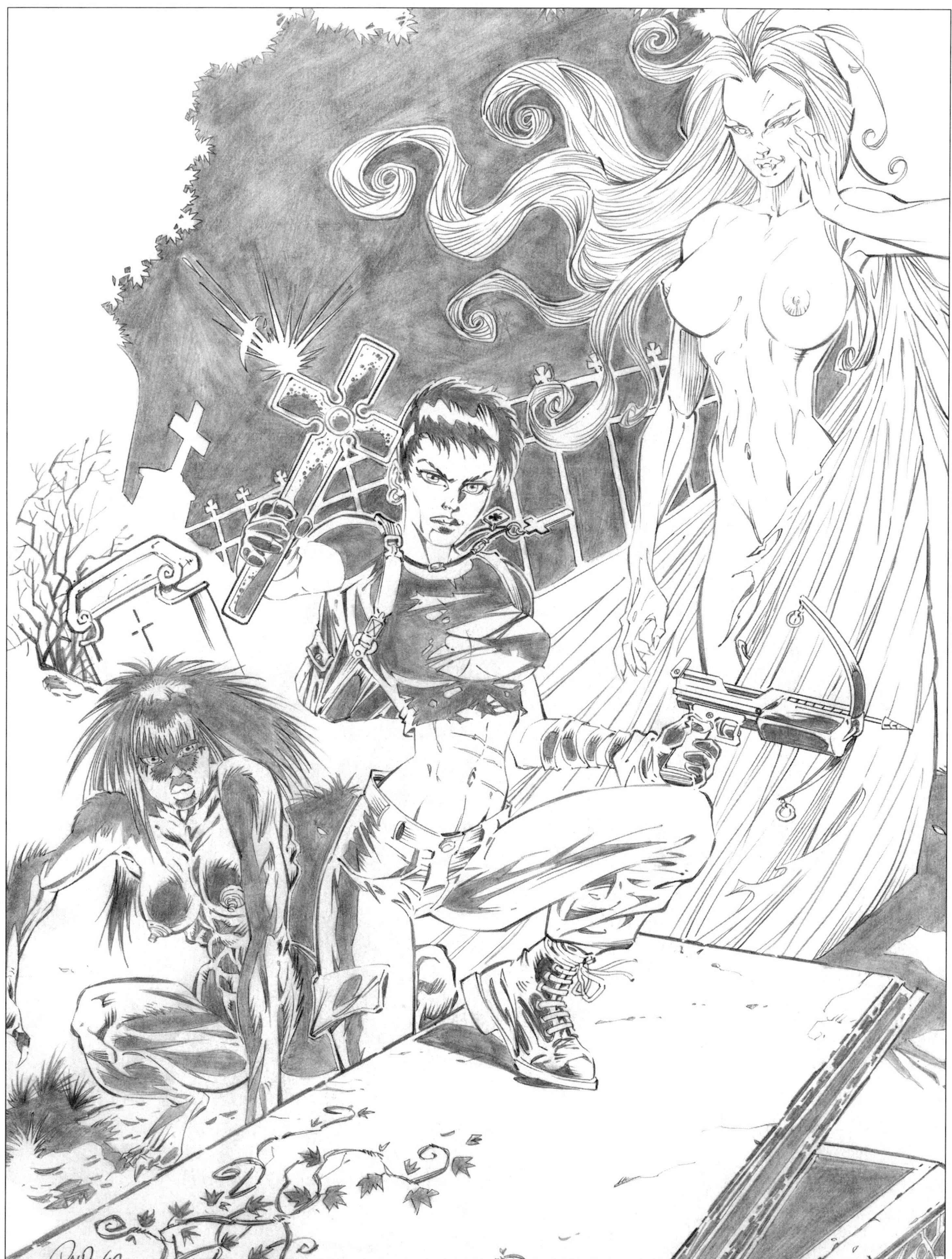

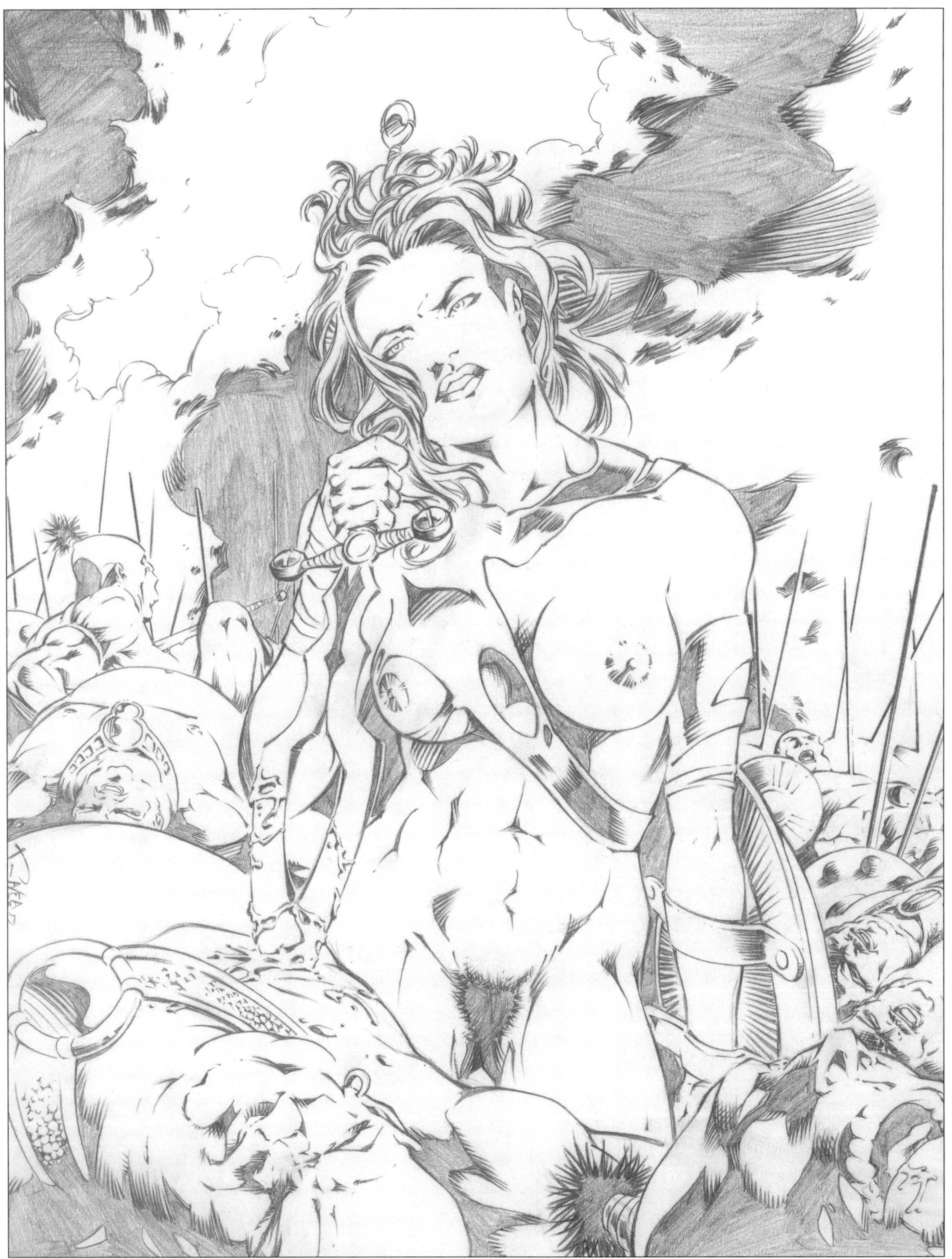

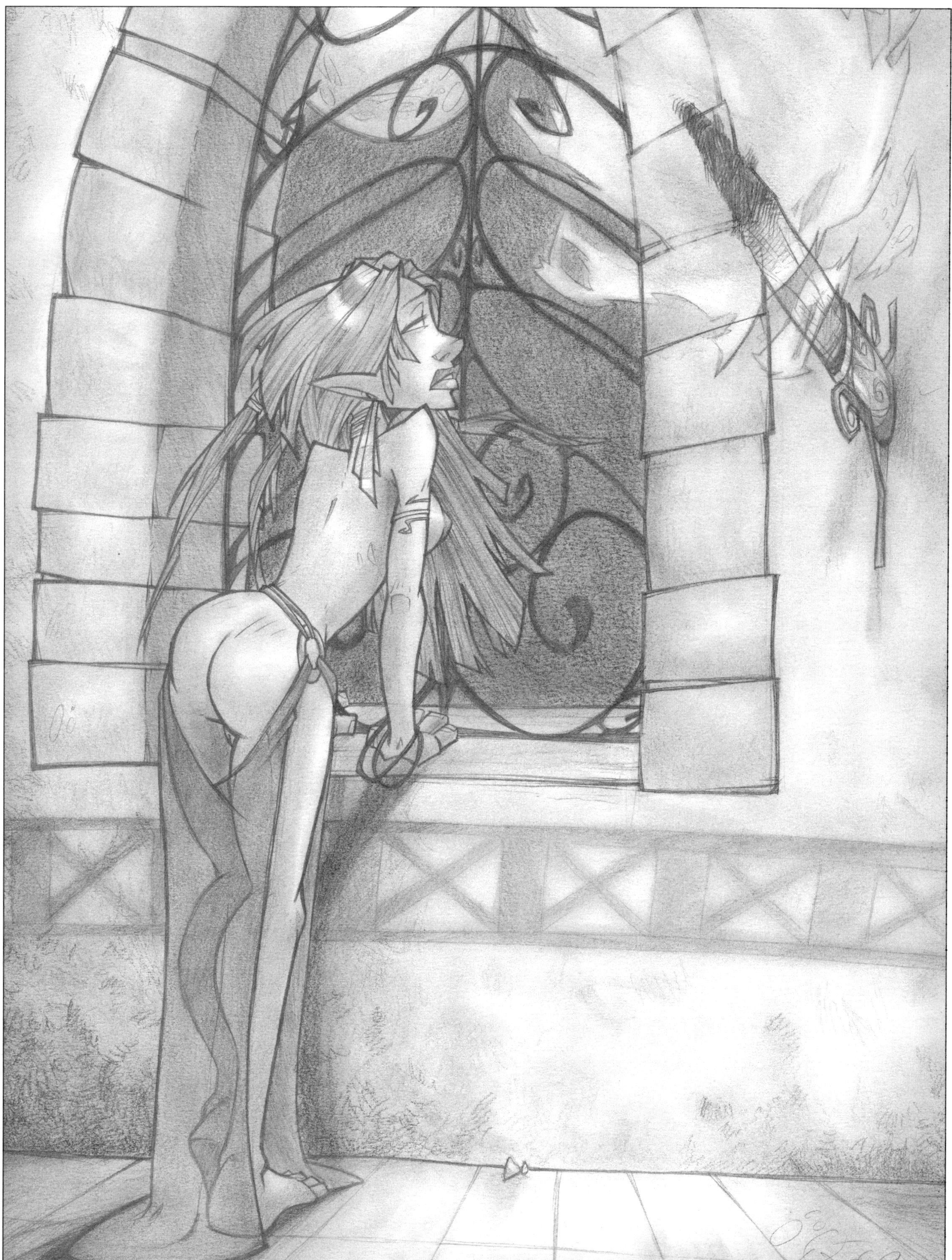

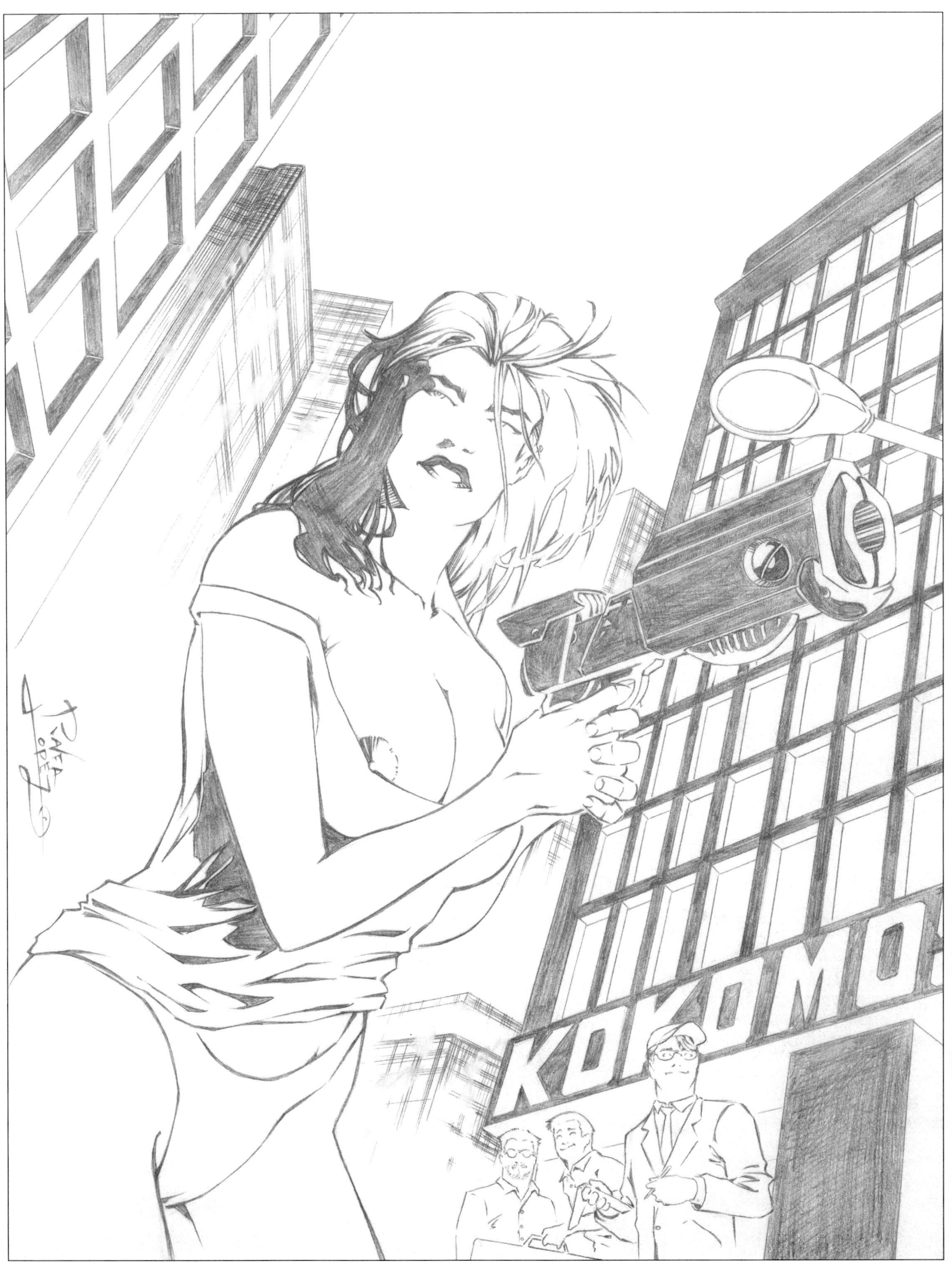
KOKOMO

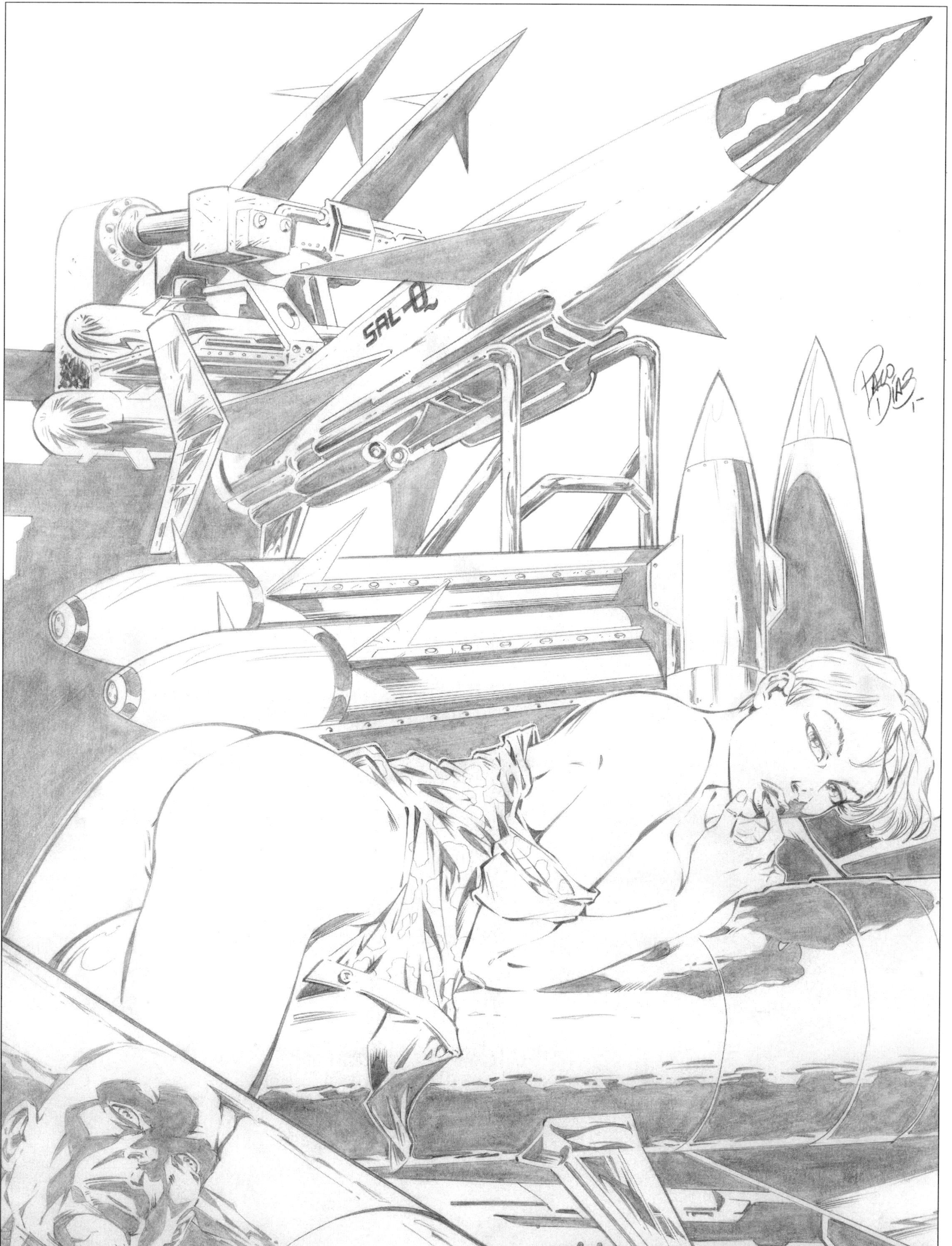
SAL-Q

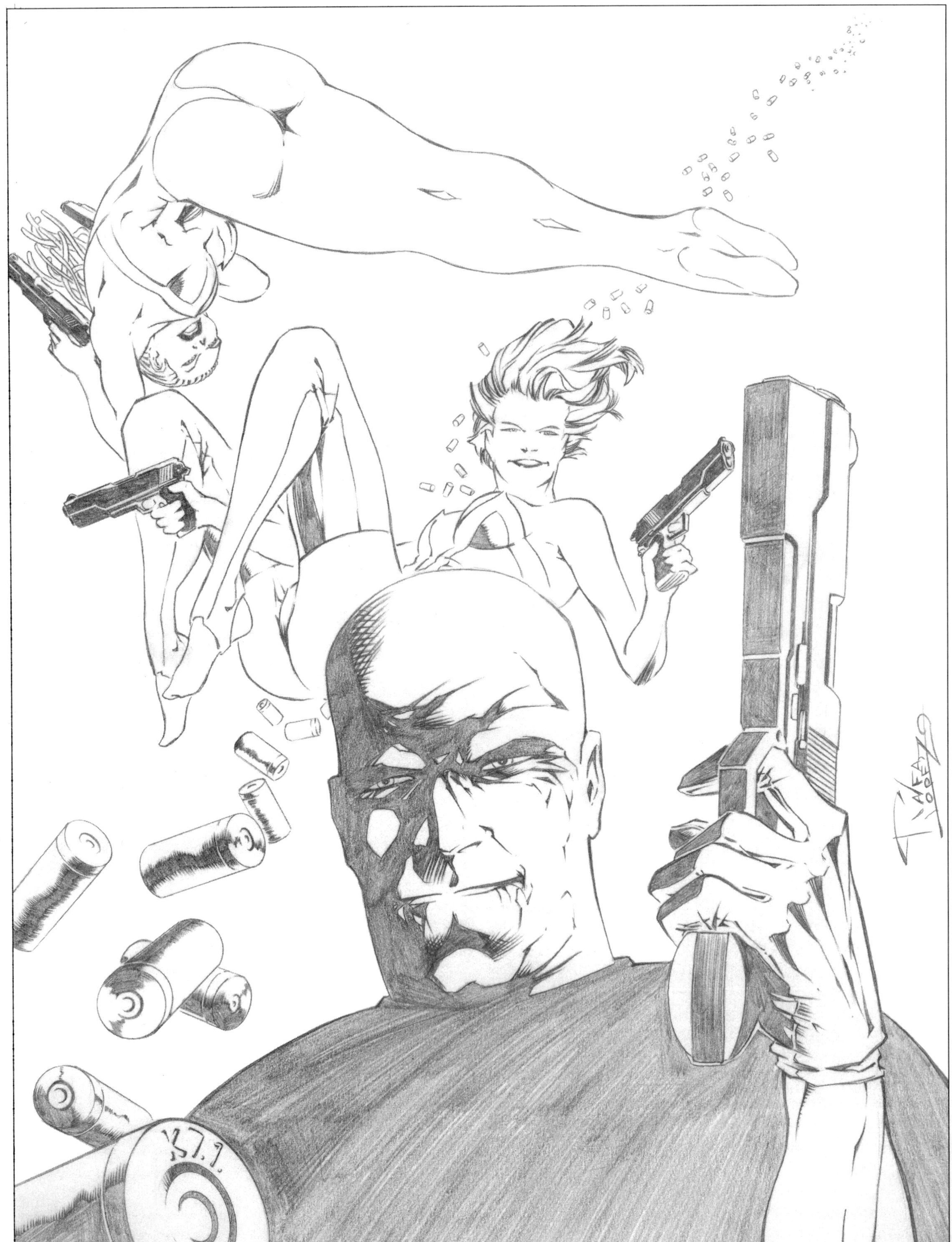

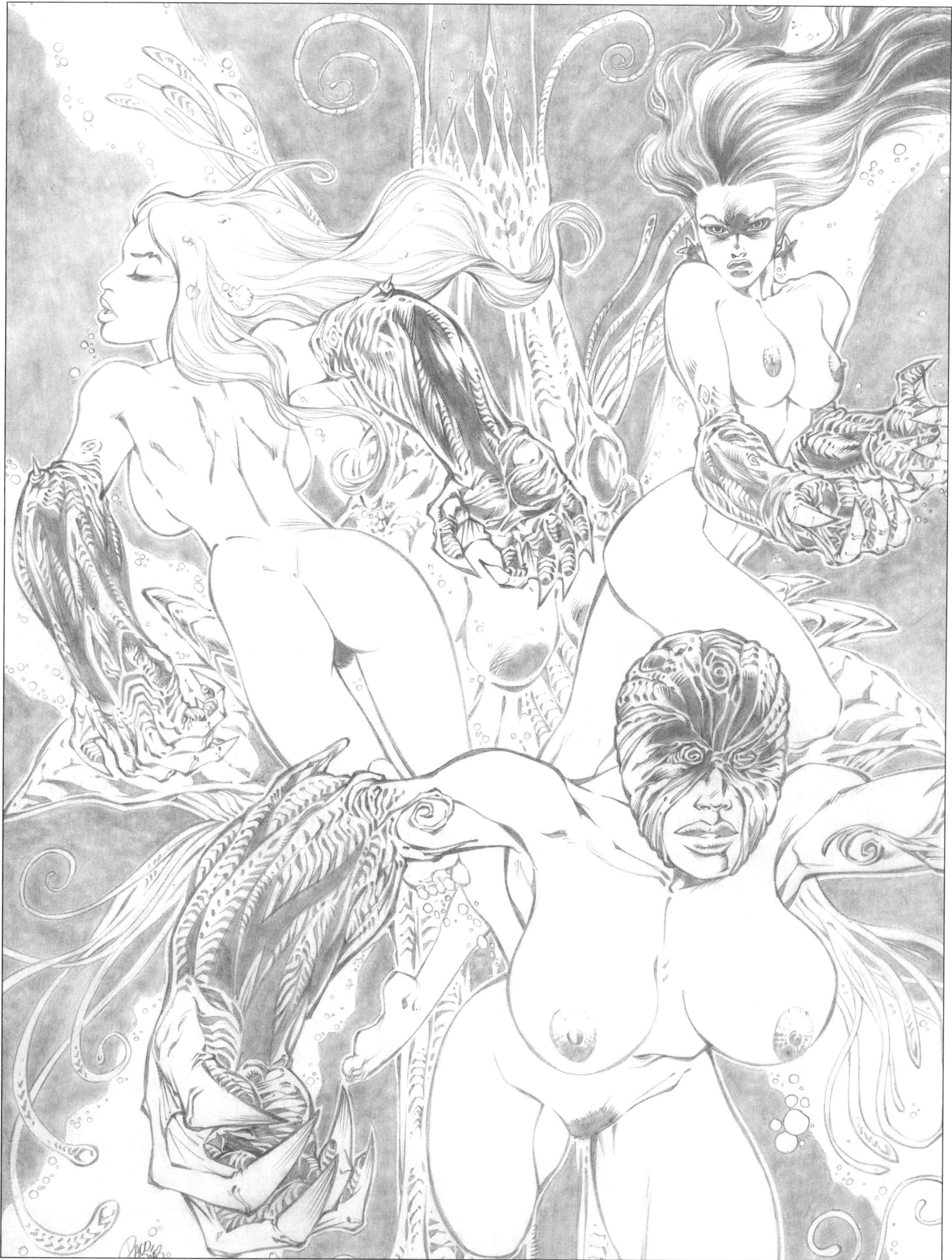

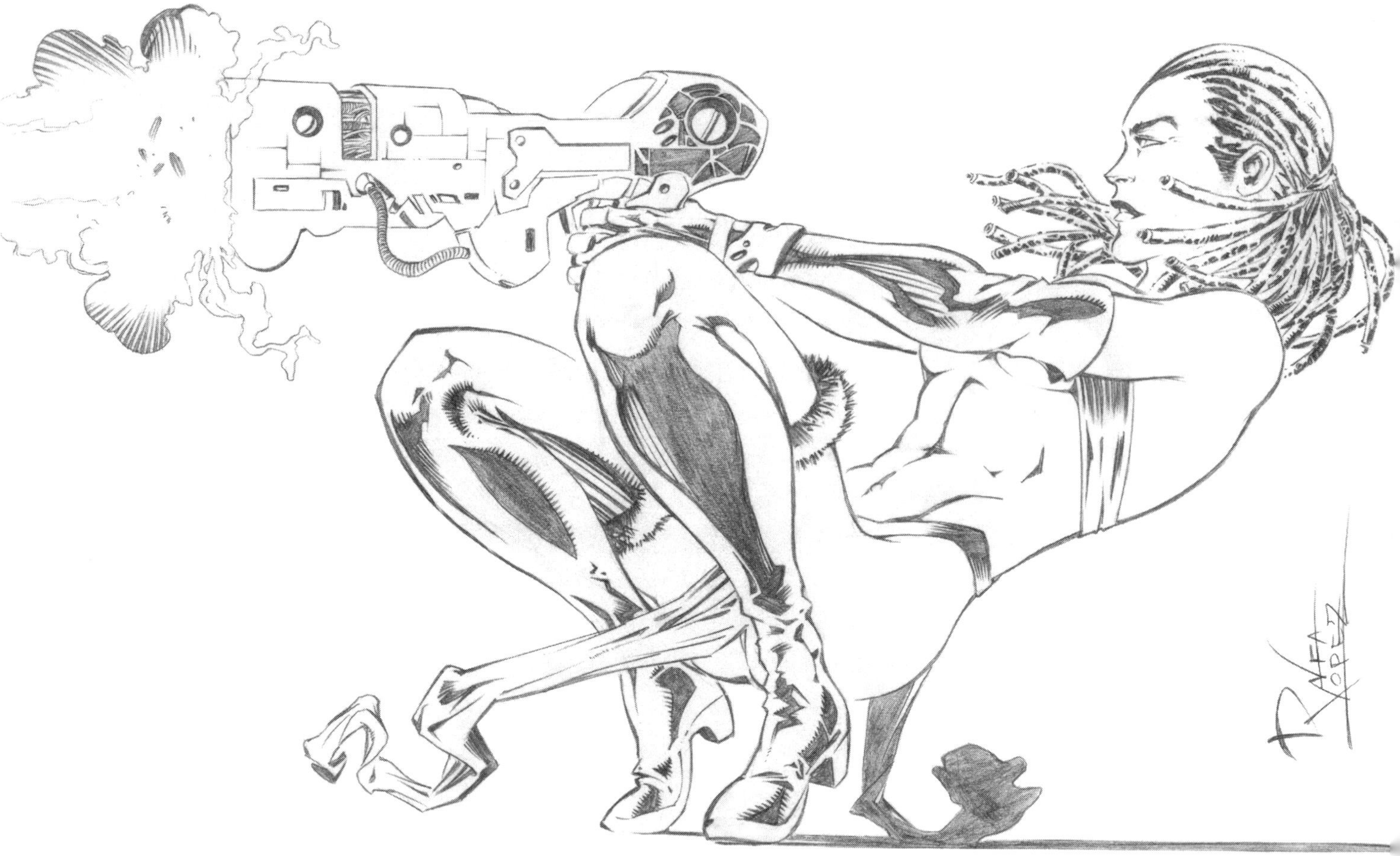

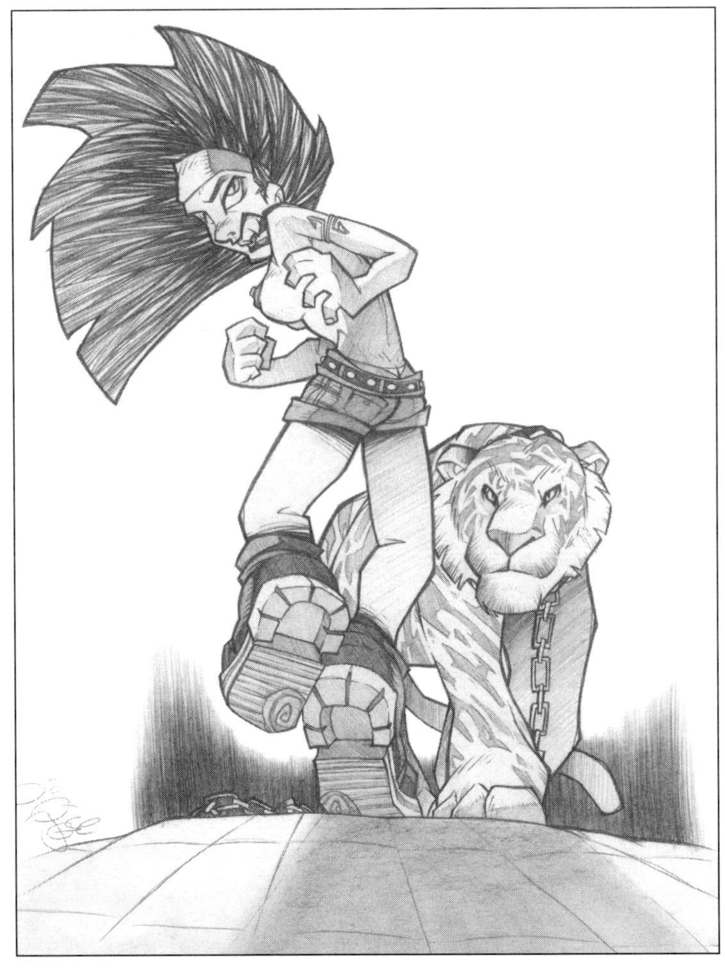

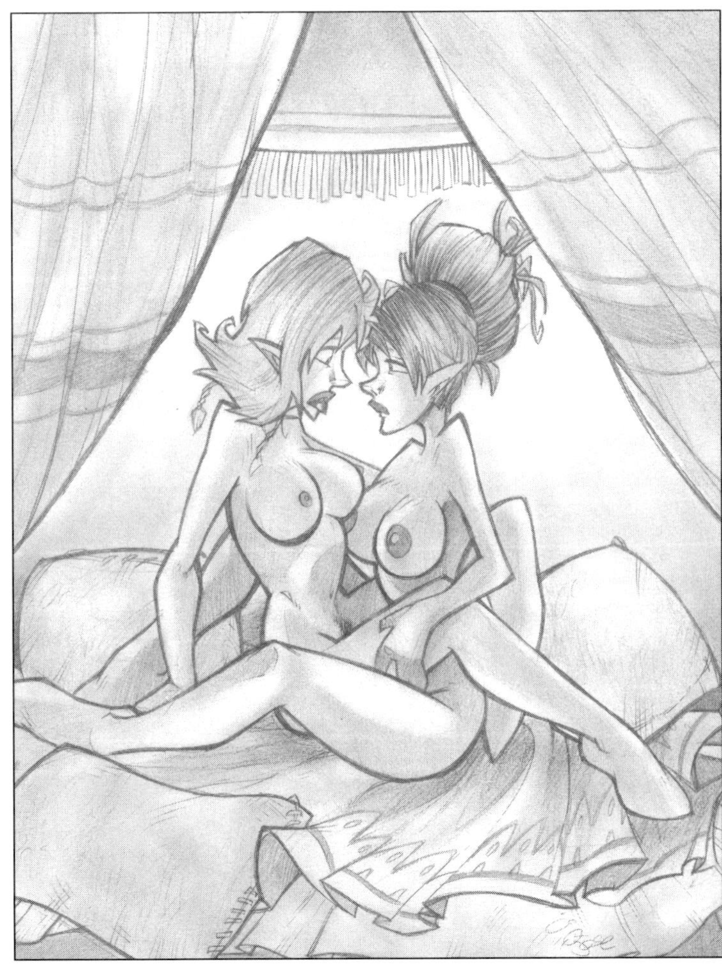

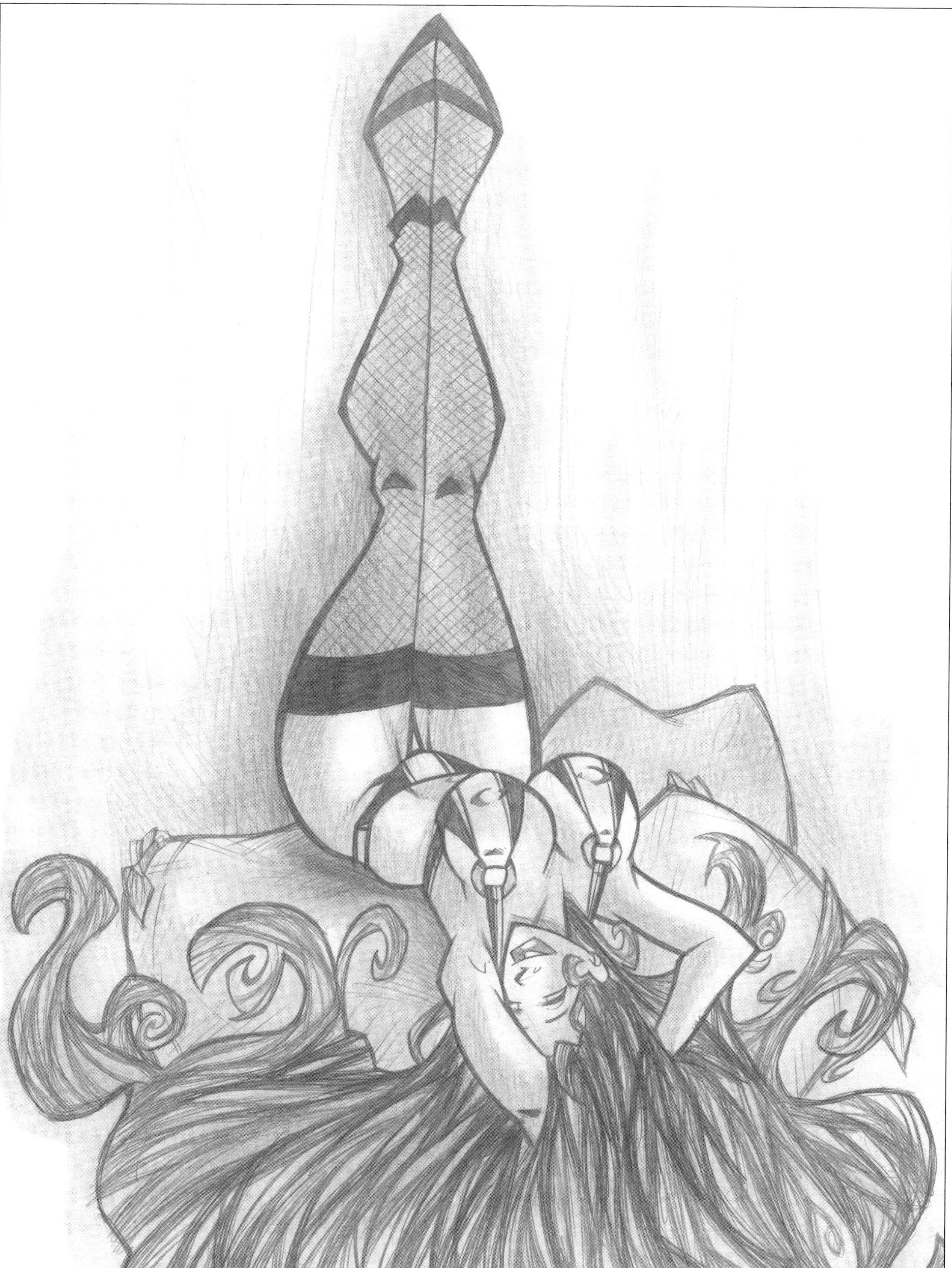

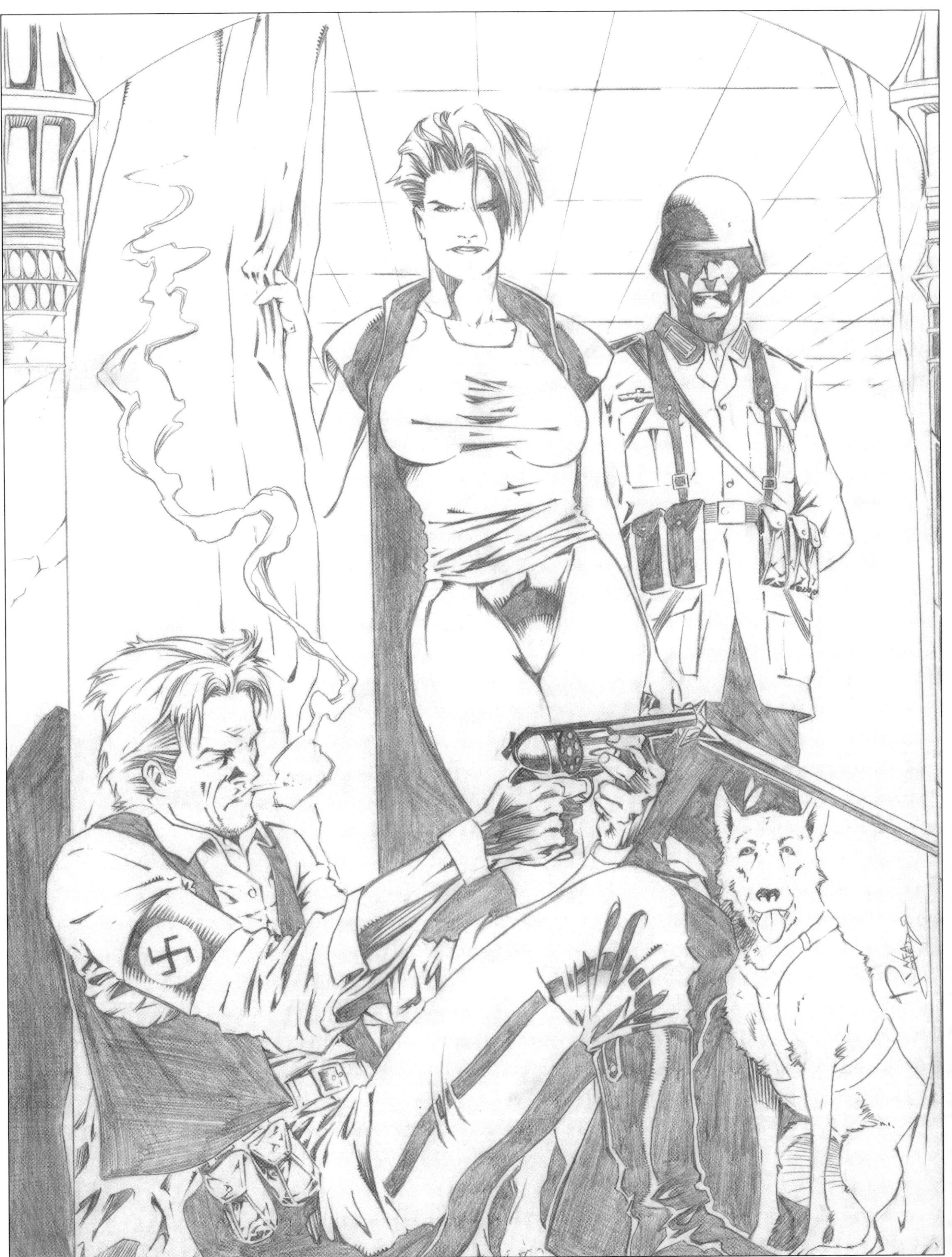

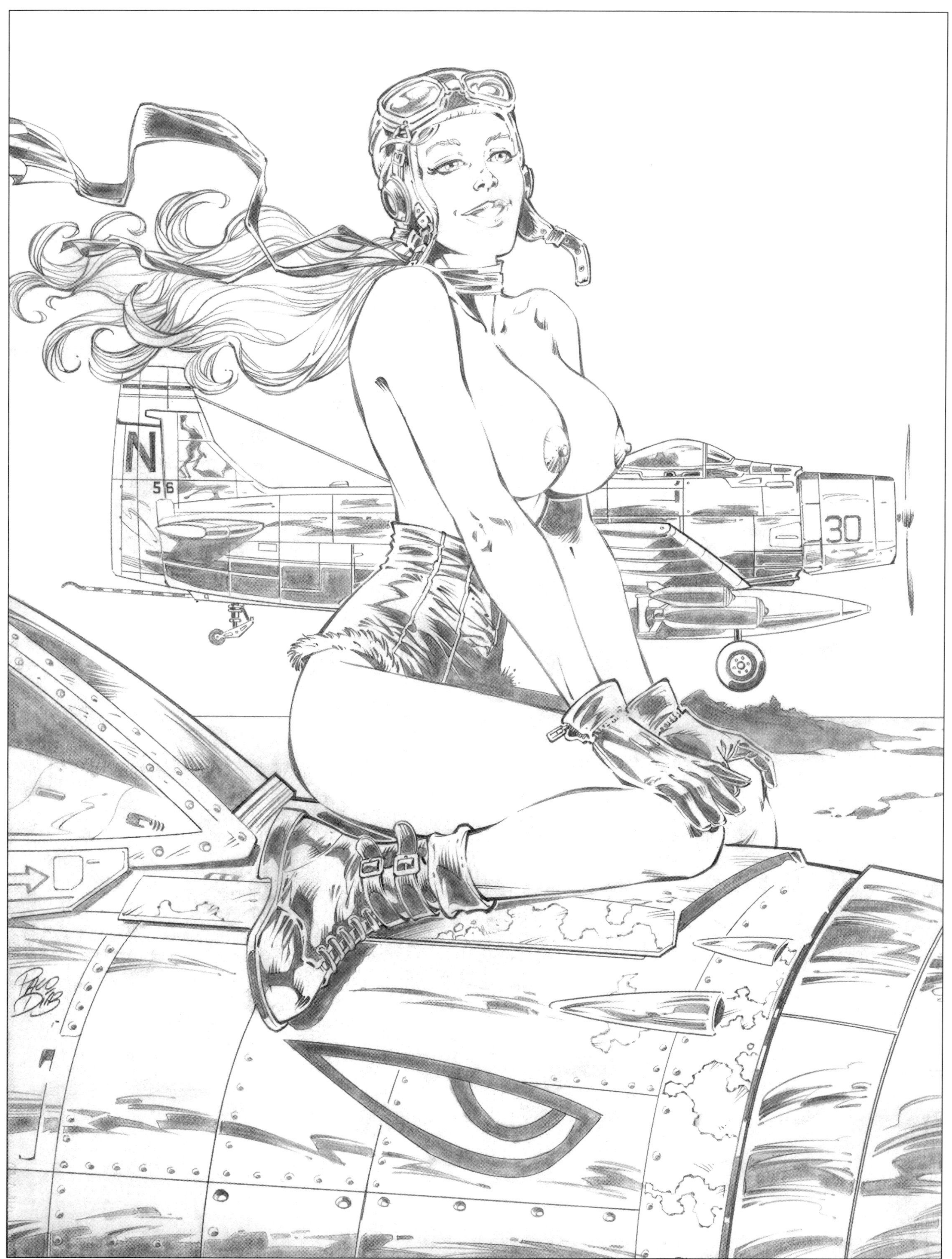
N
56
30

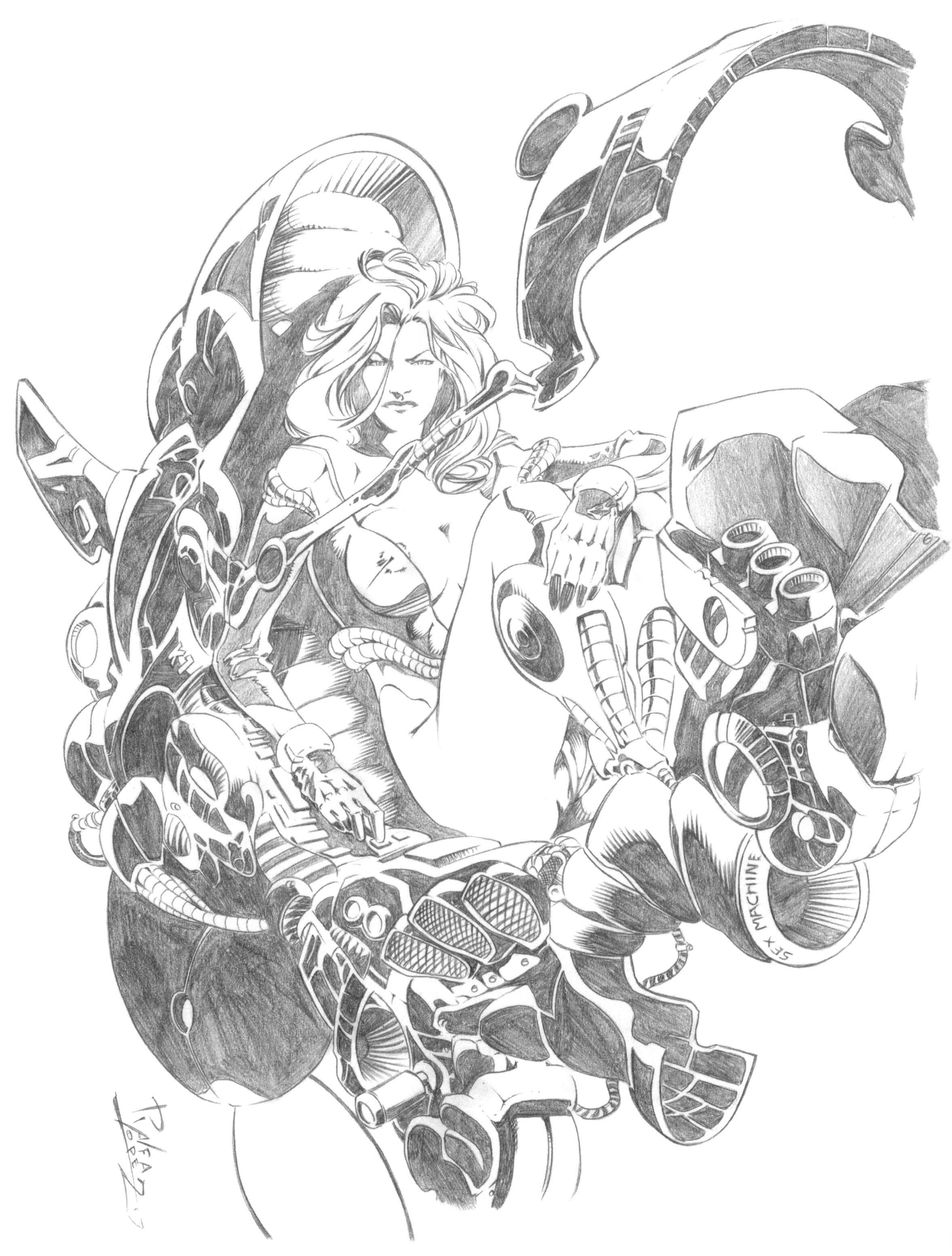
SEX MACHINE

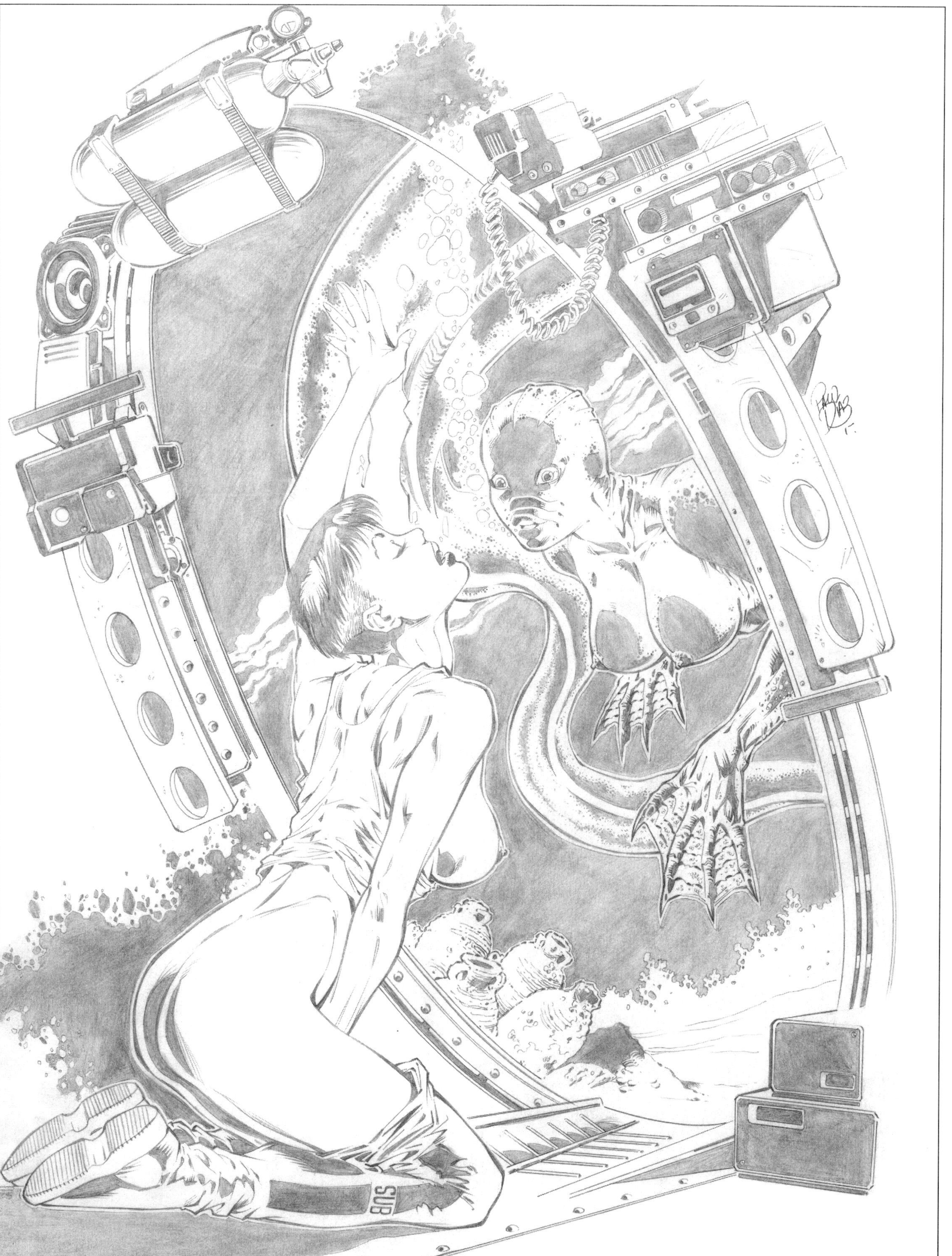
SUB

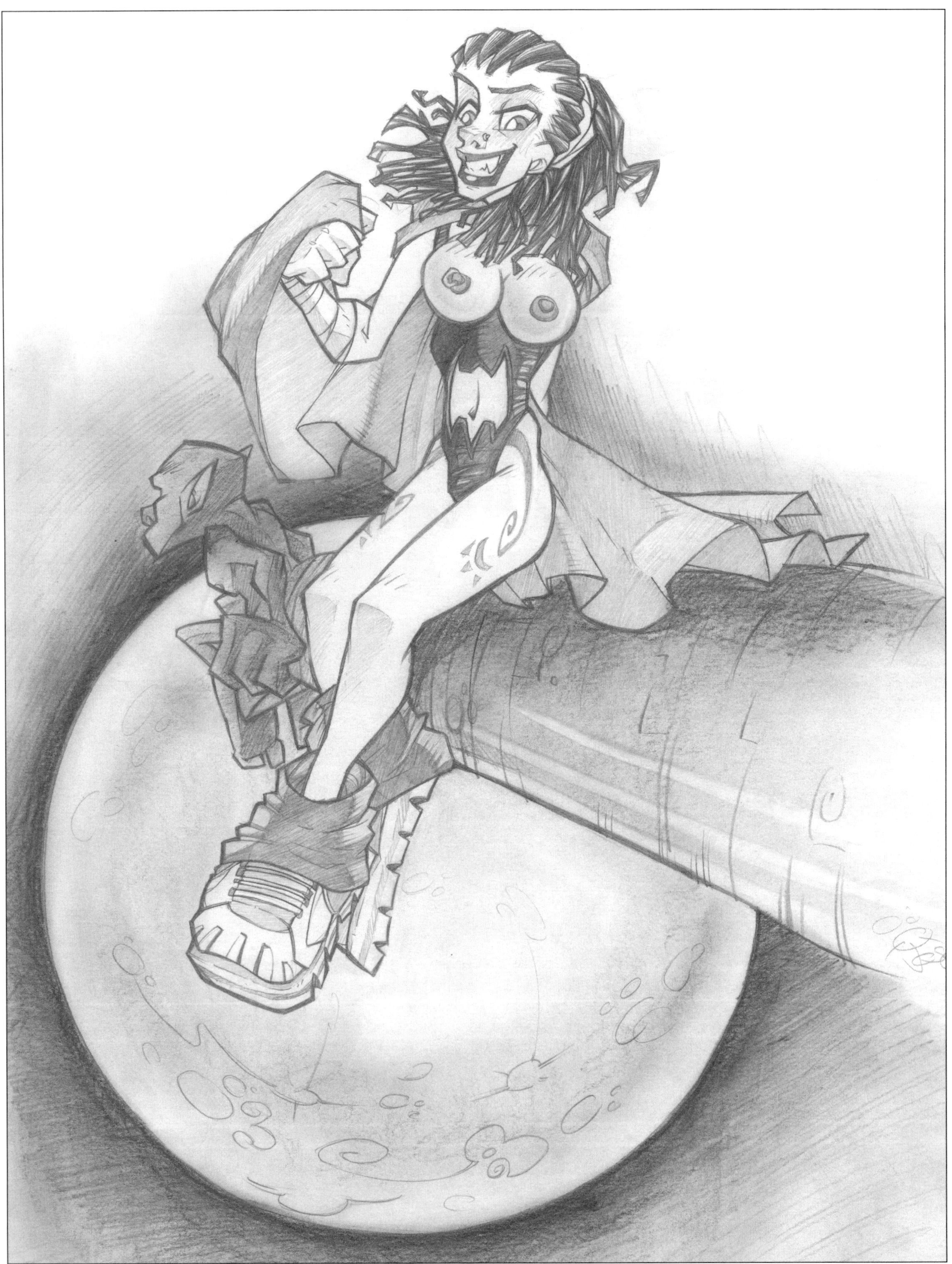

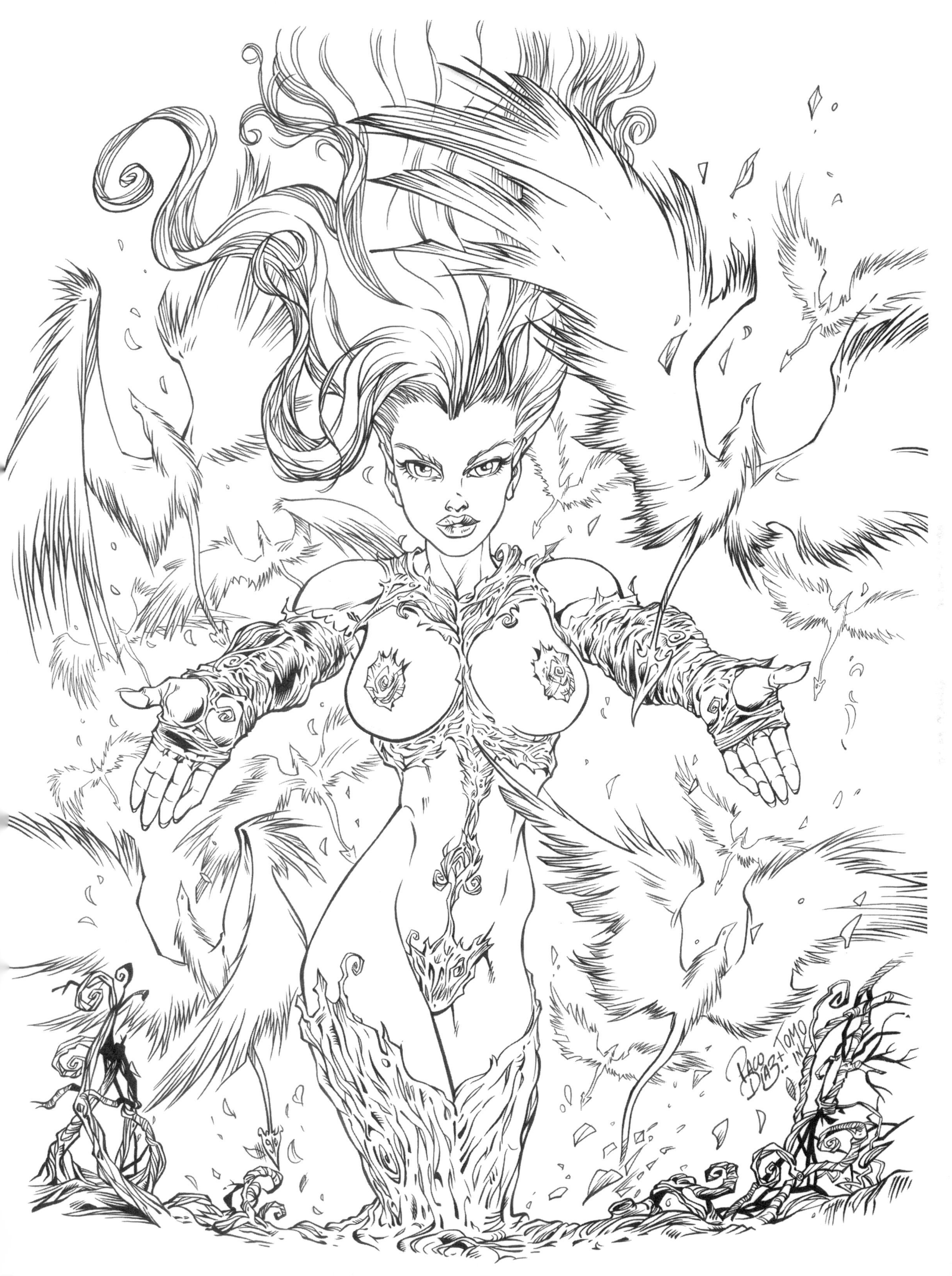
PACO DIAZ + TOMO INK

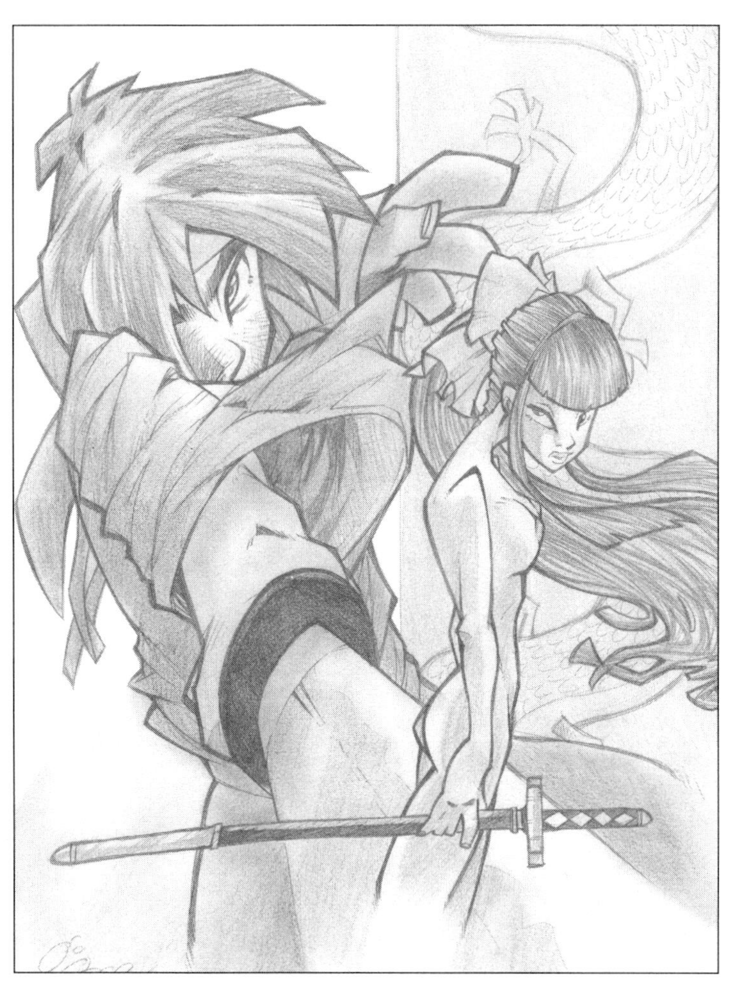

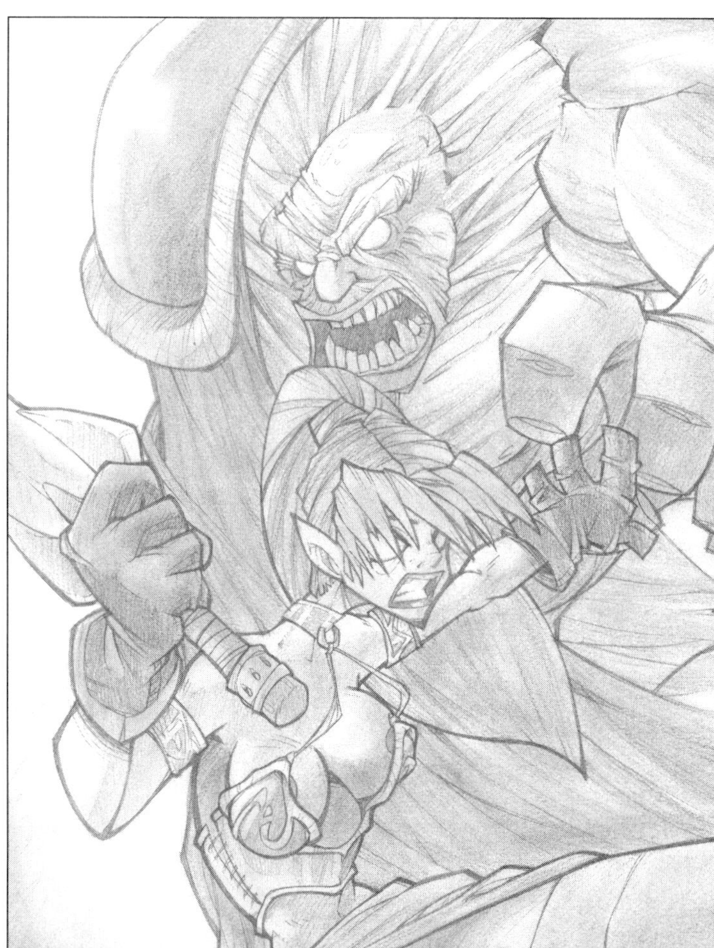

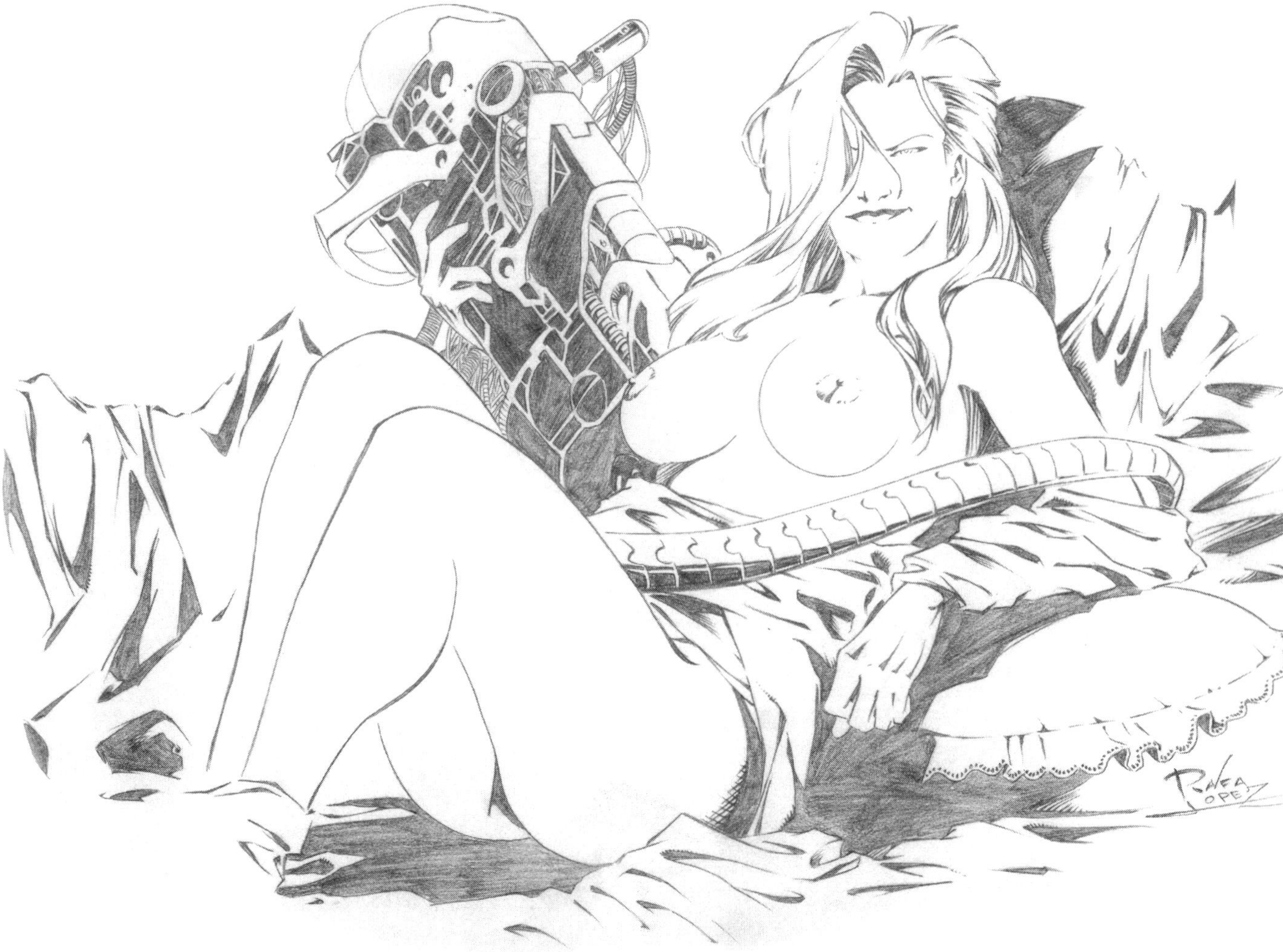

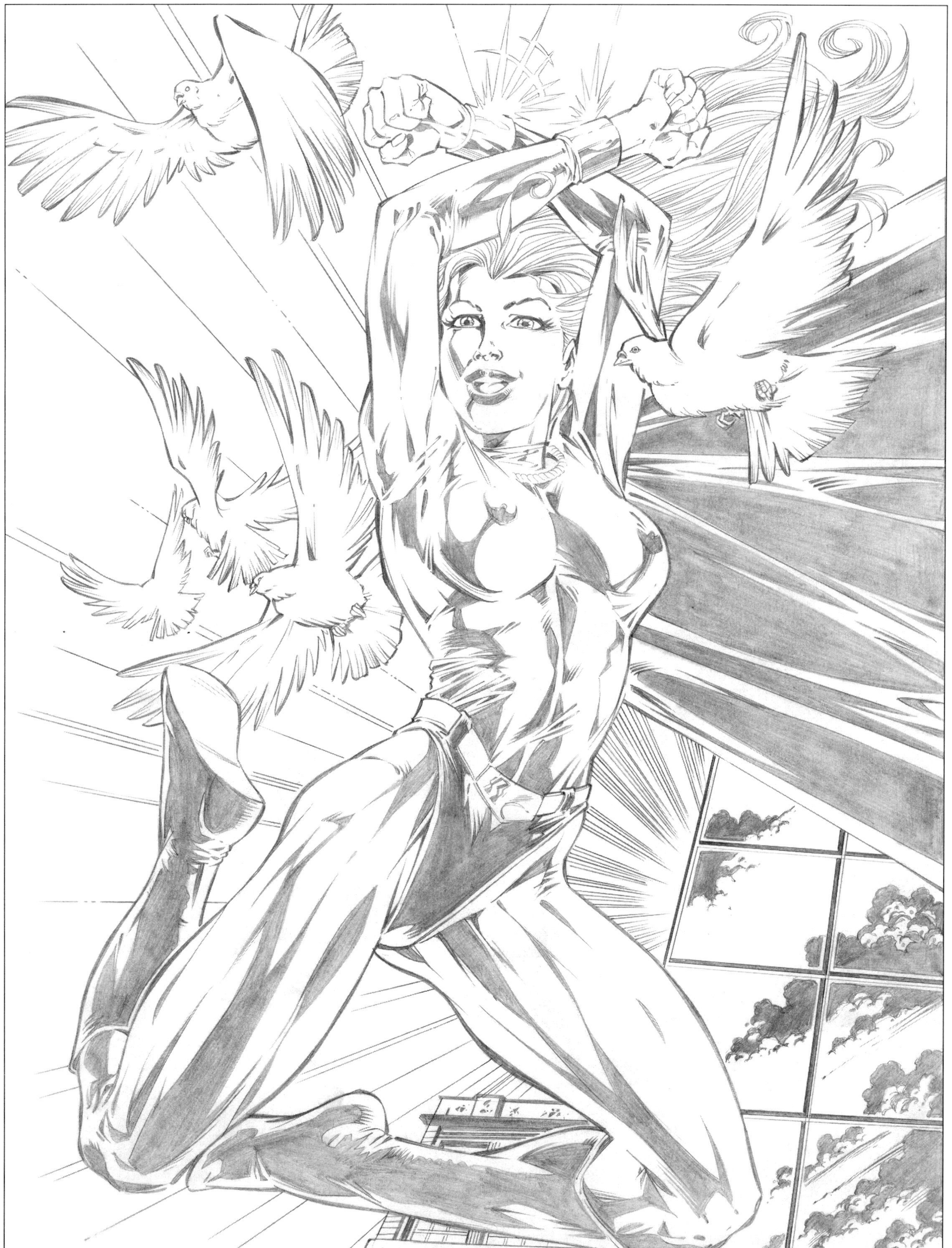

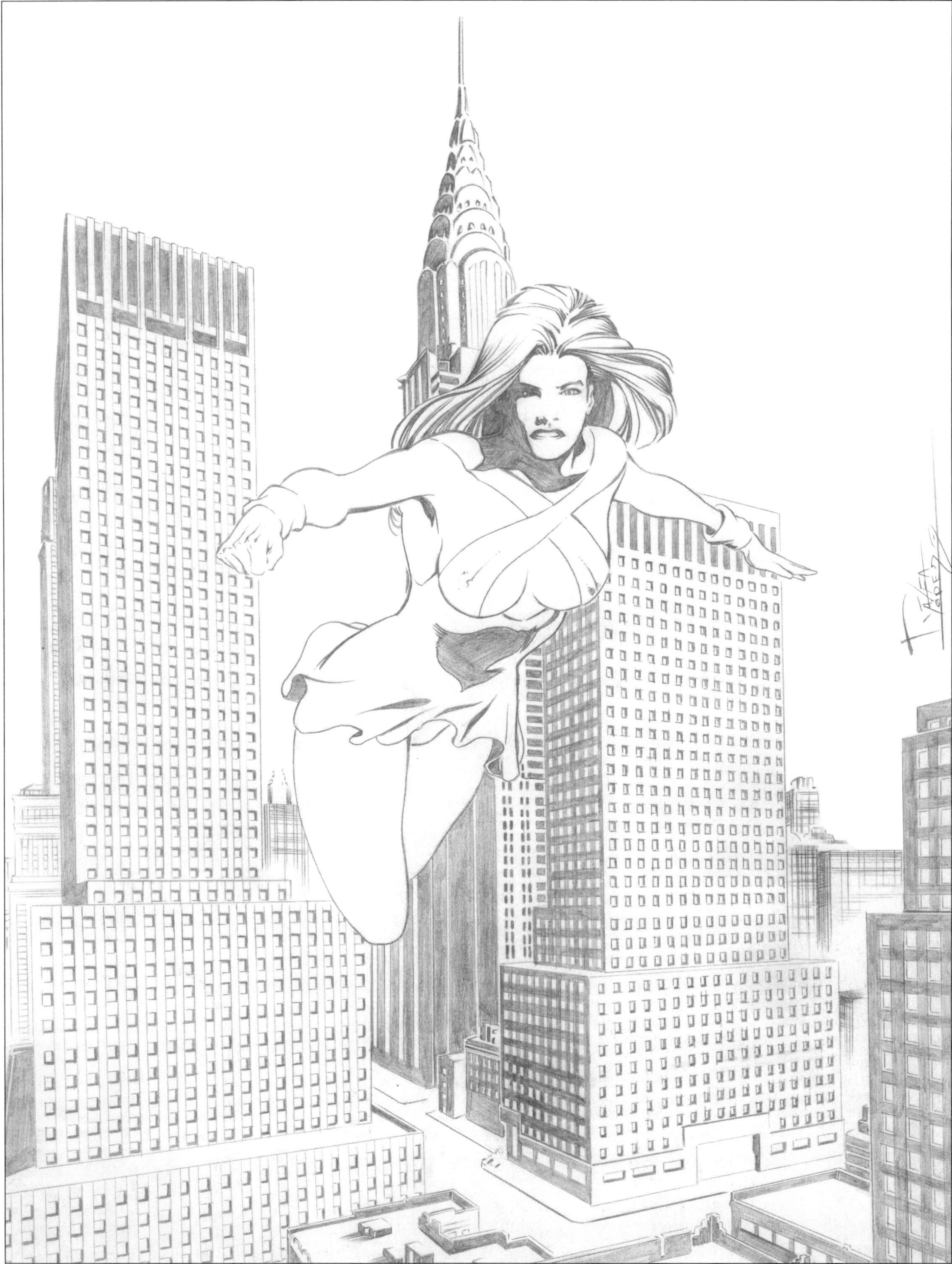

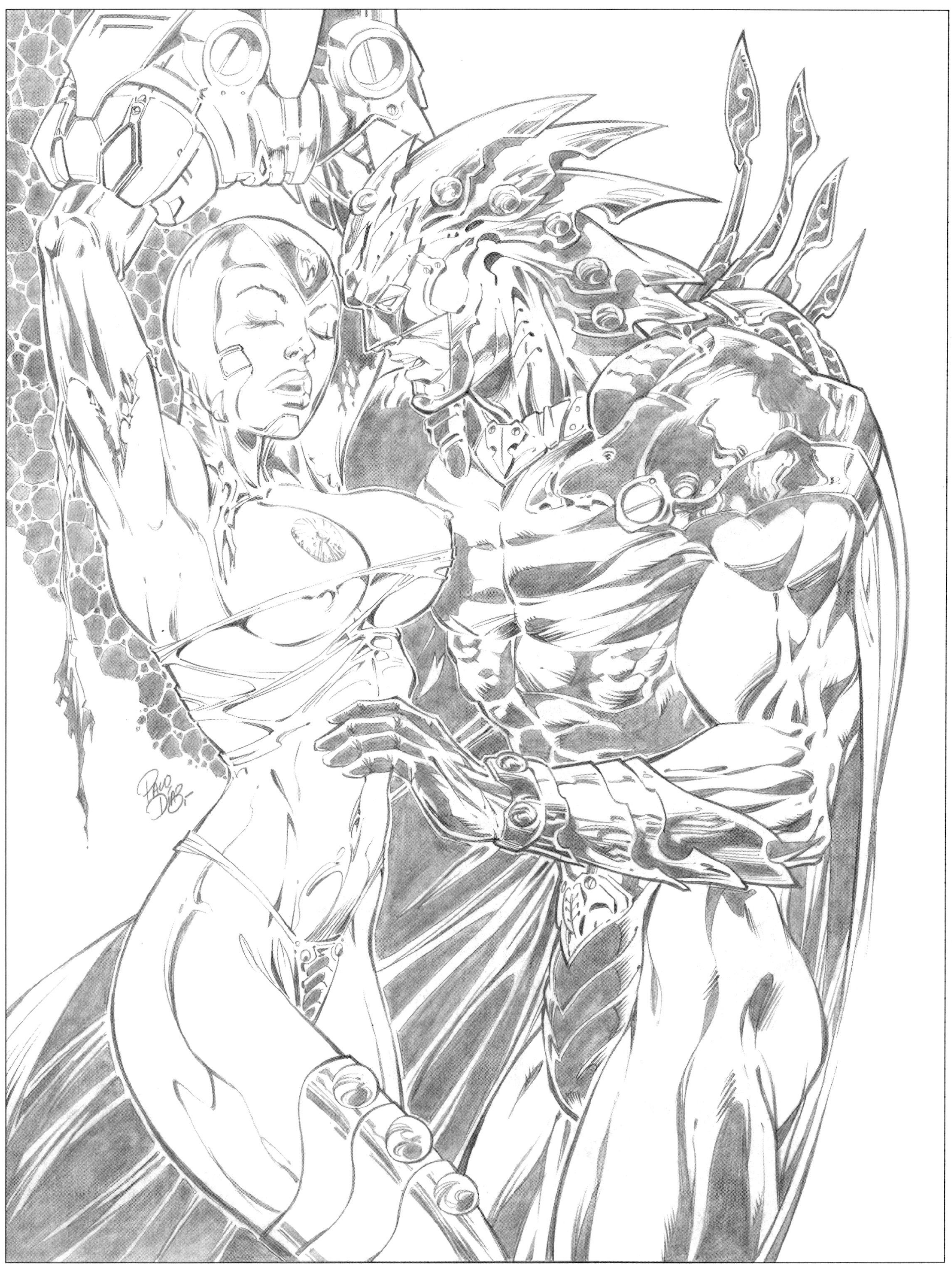

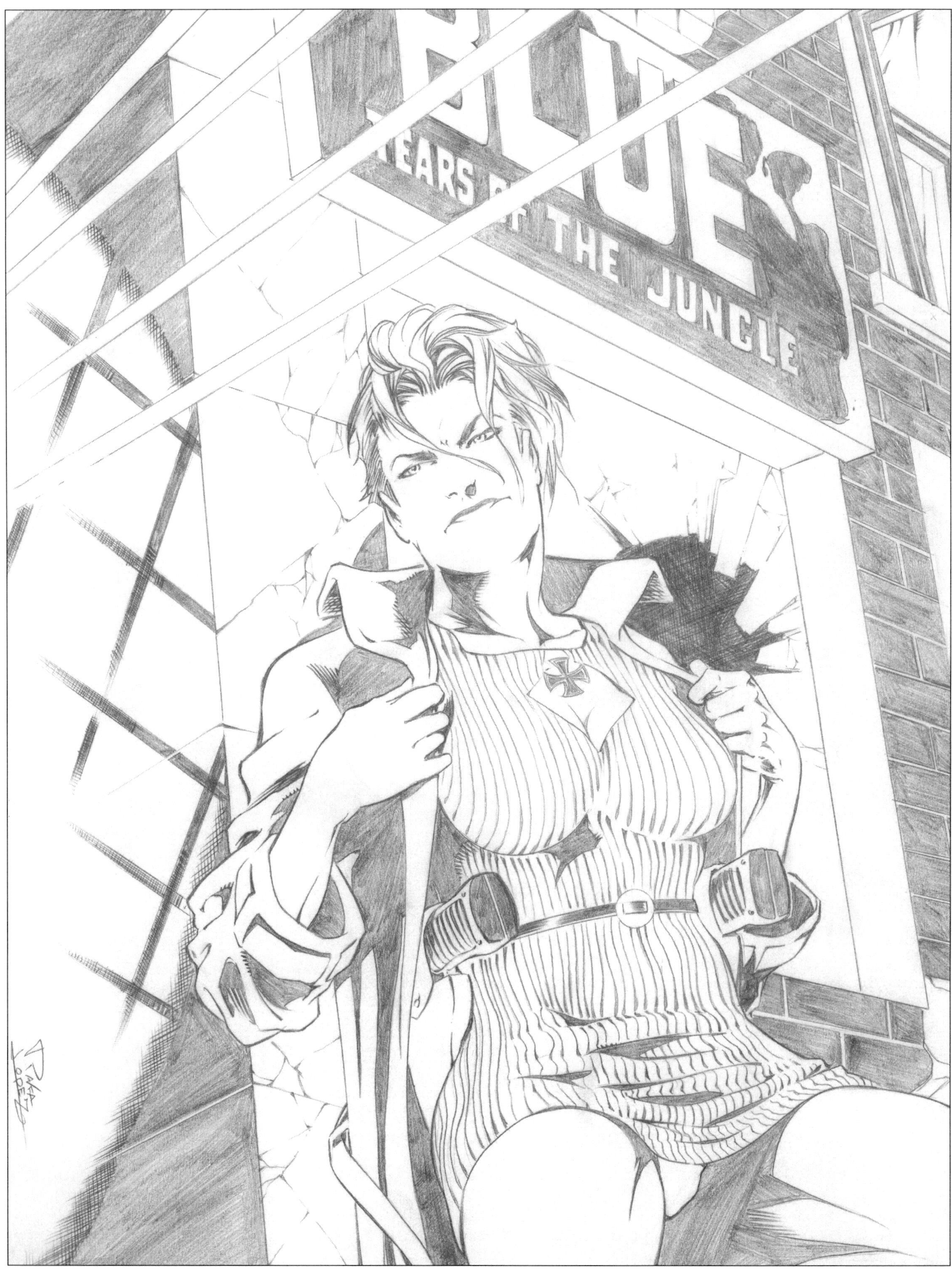

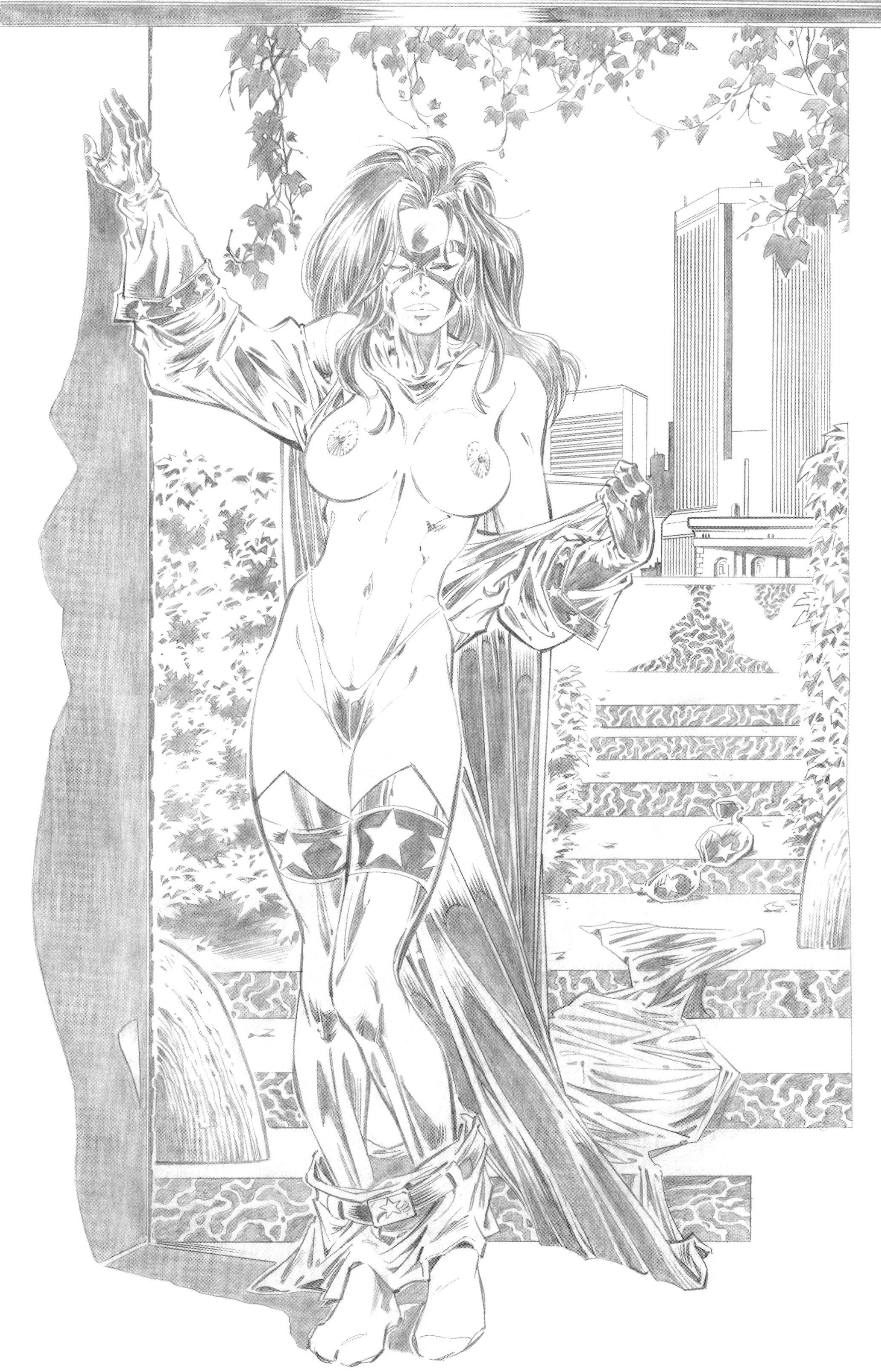

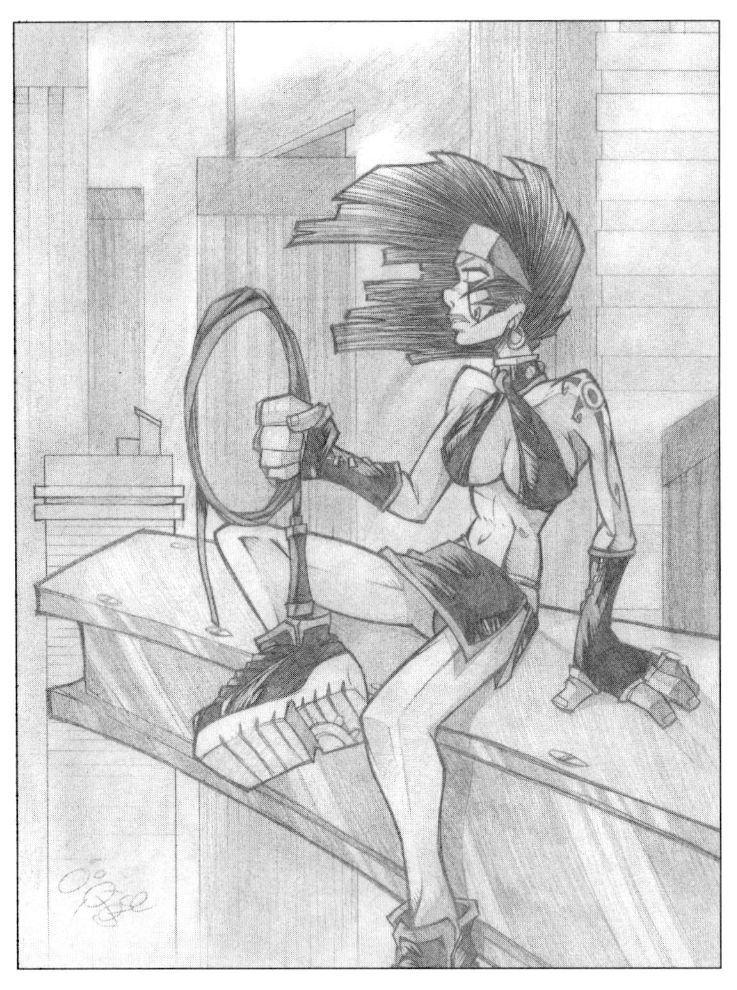

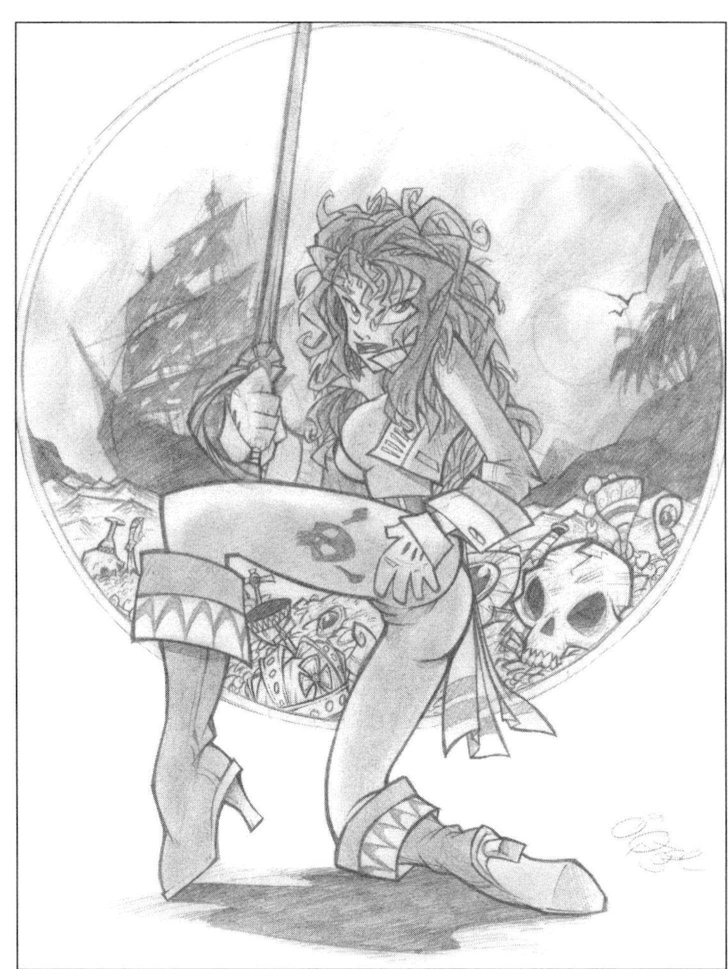

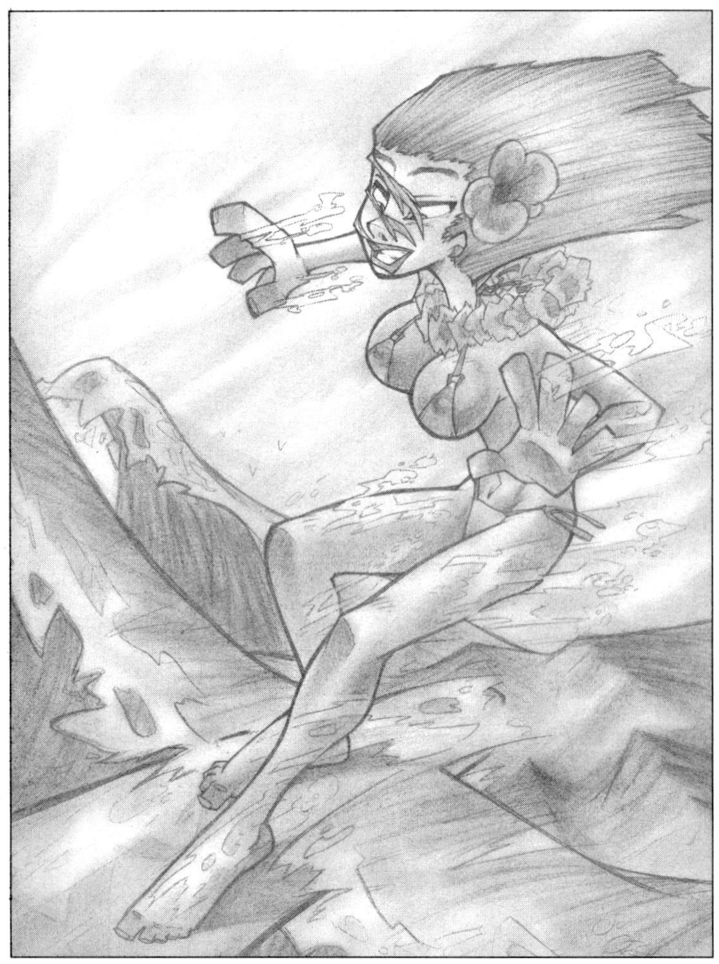

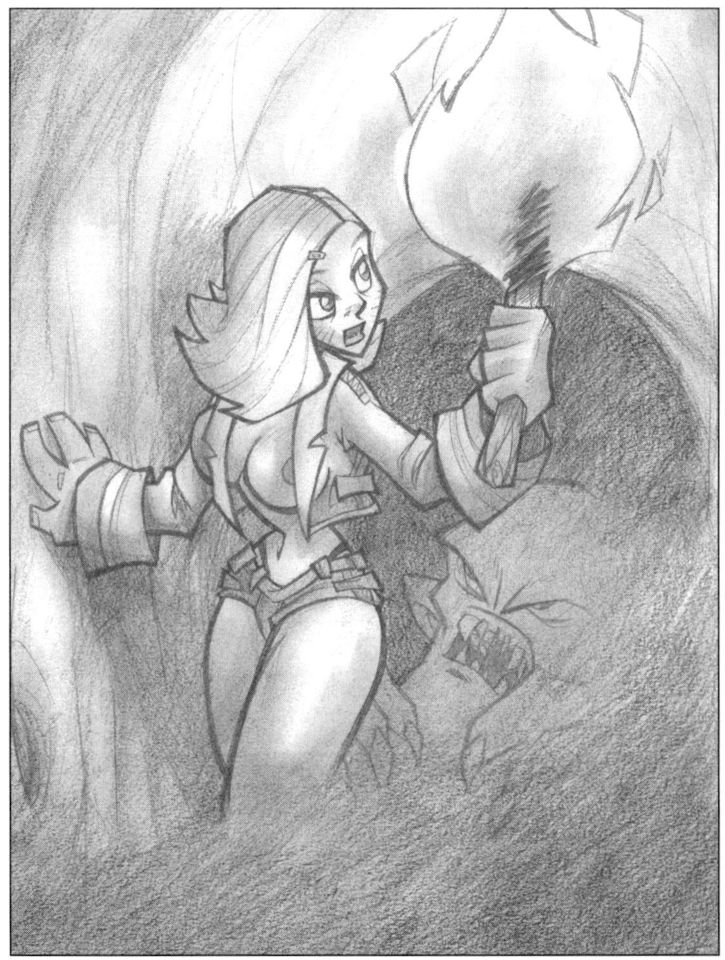

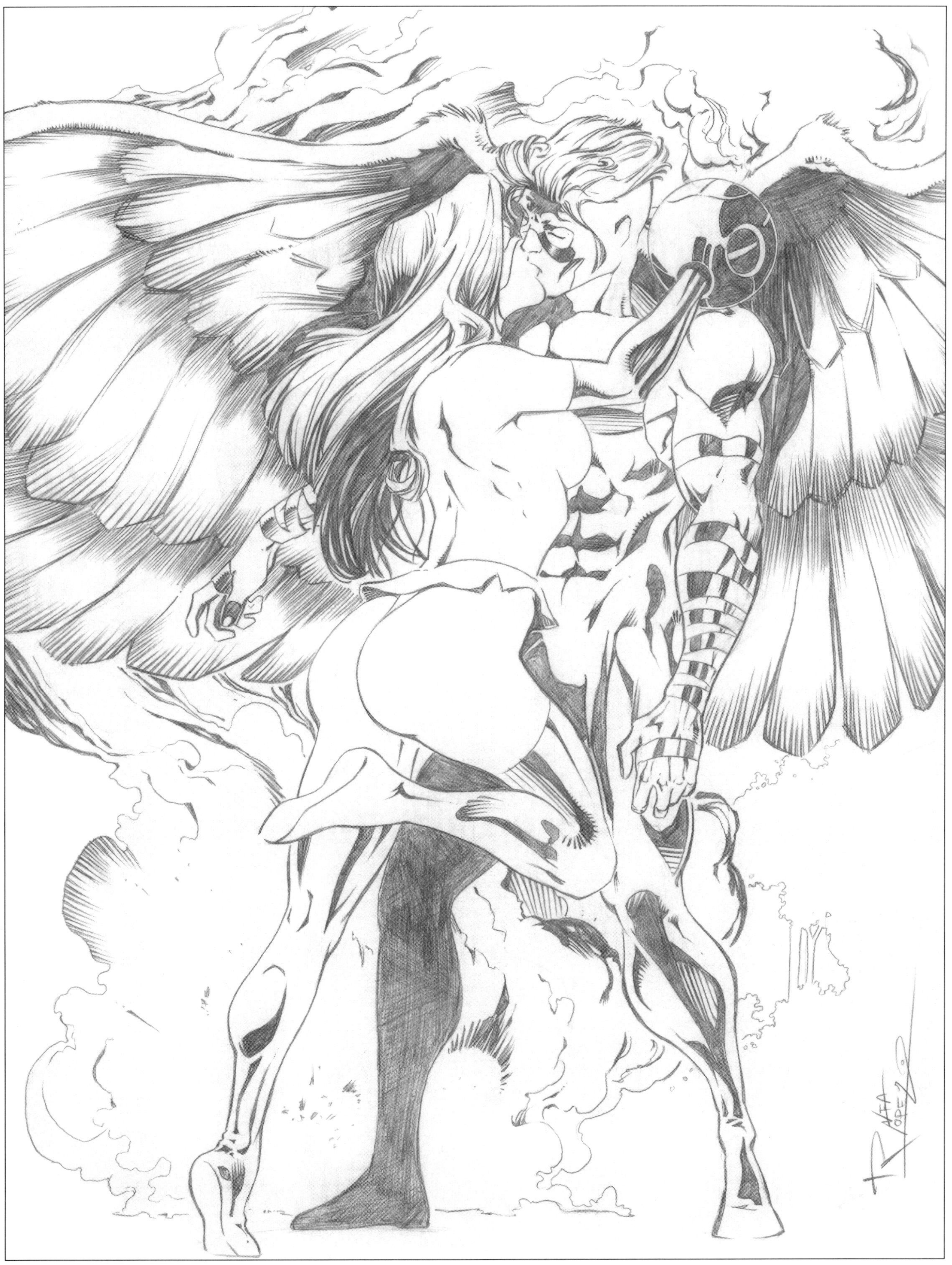

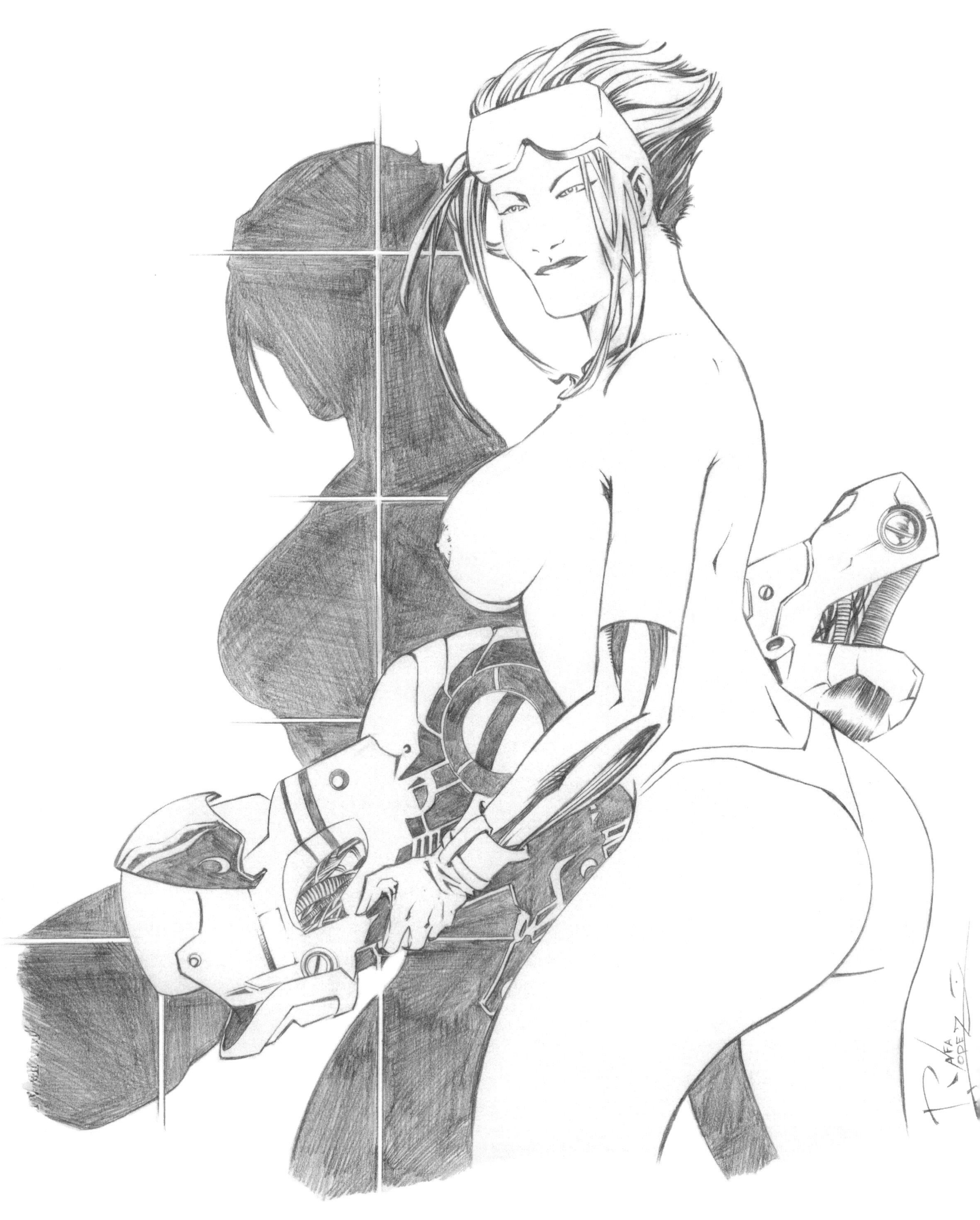

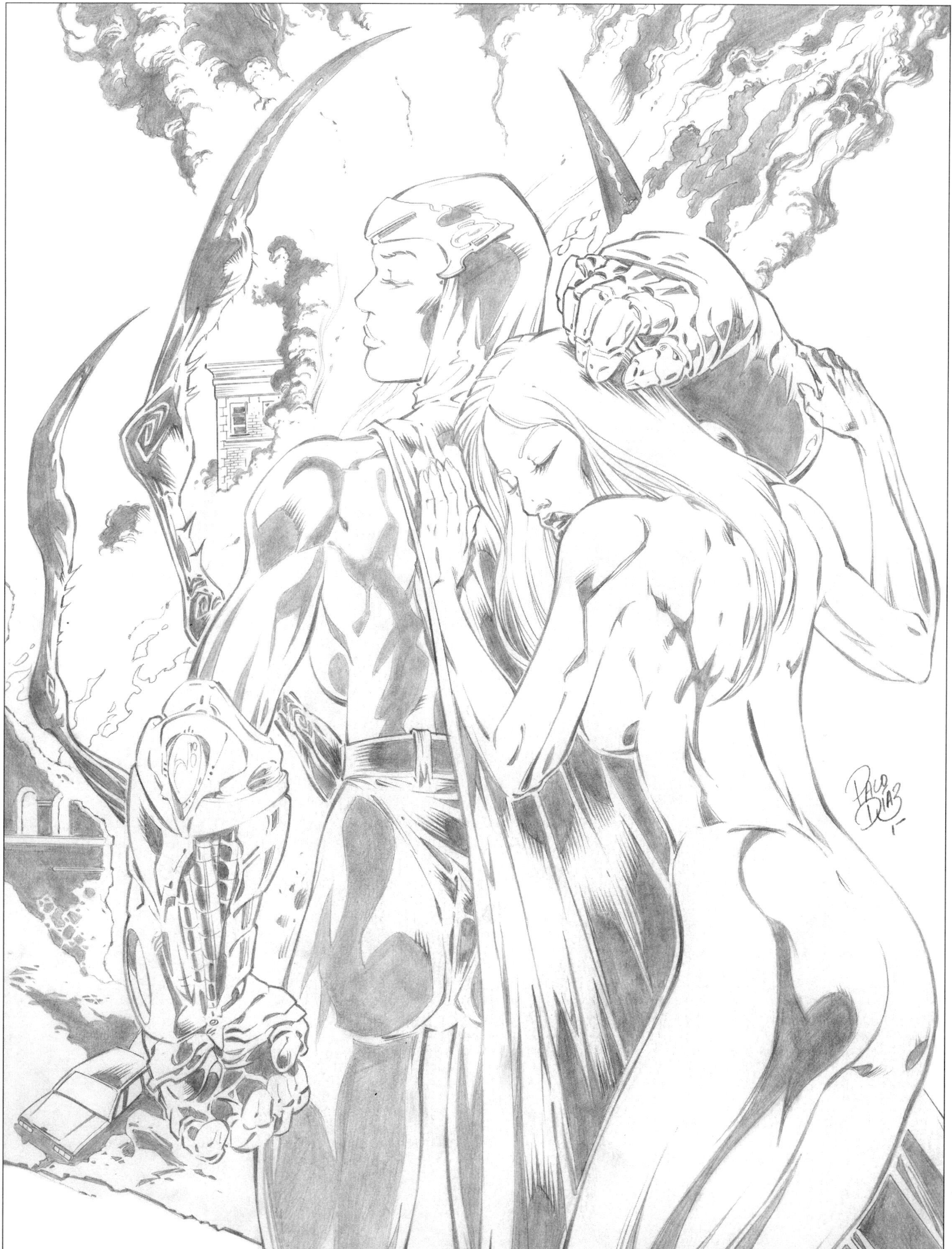

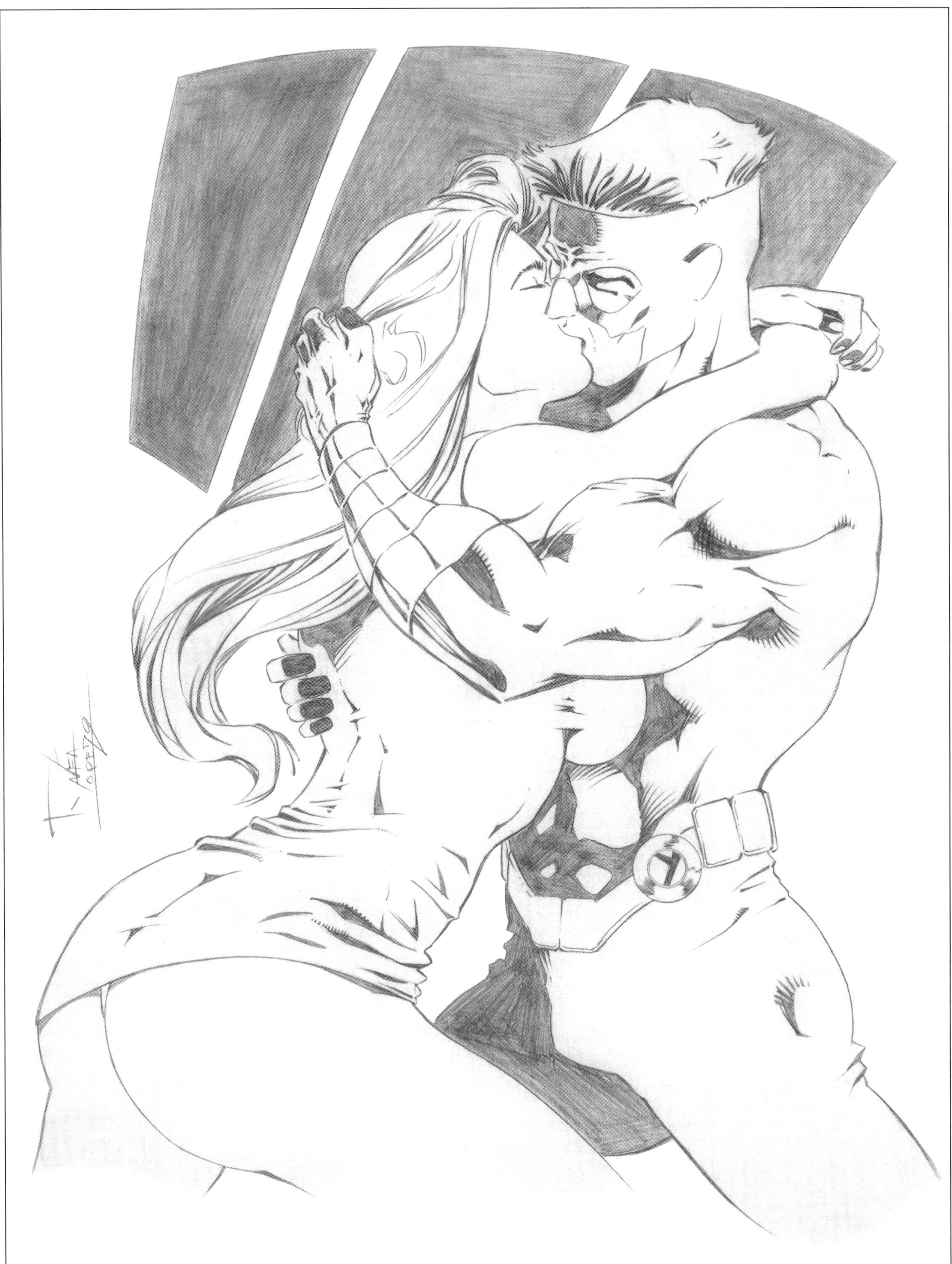

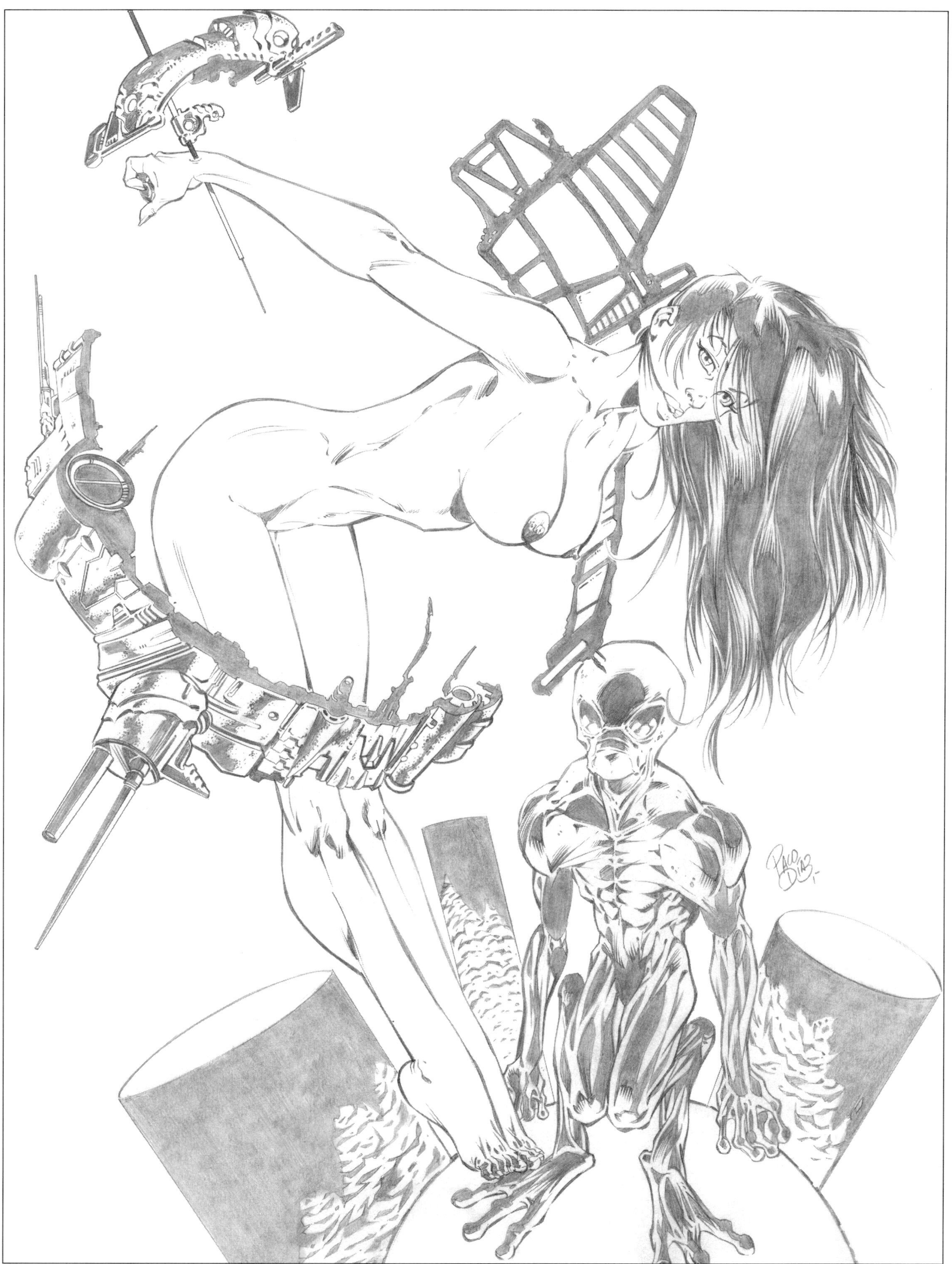

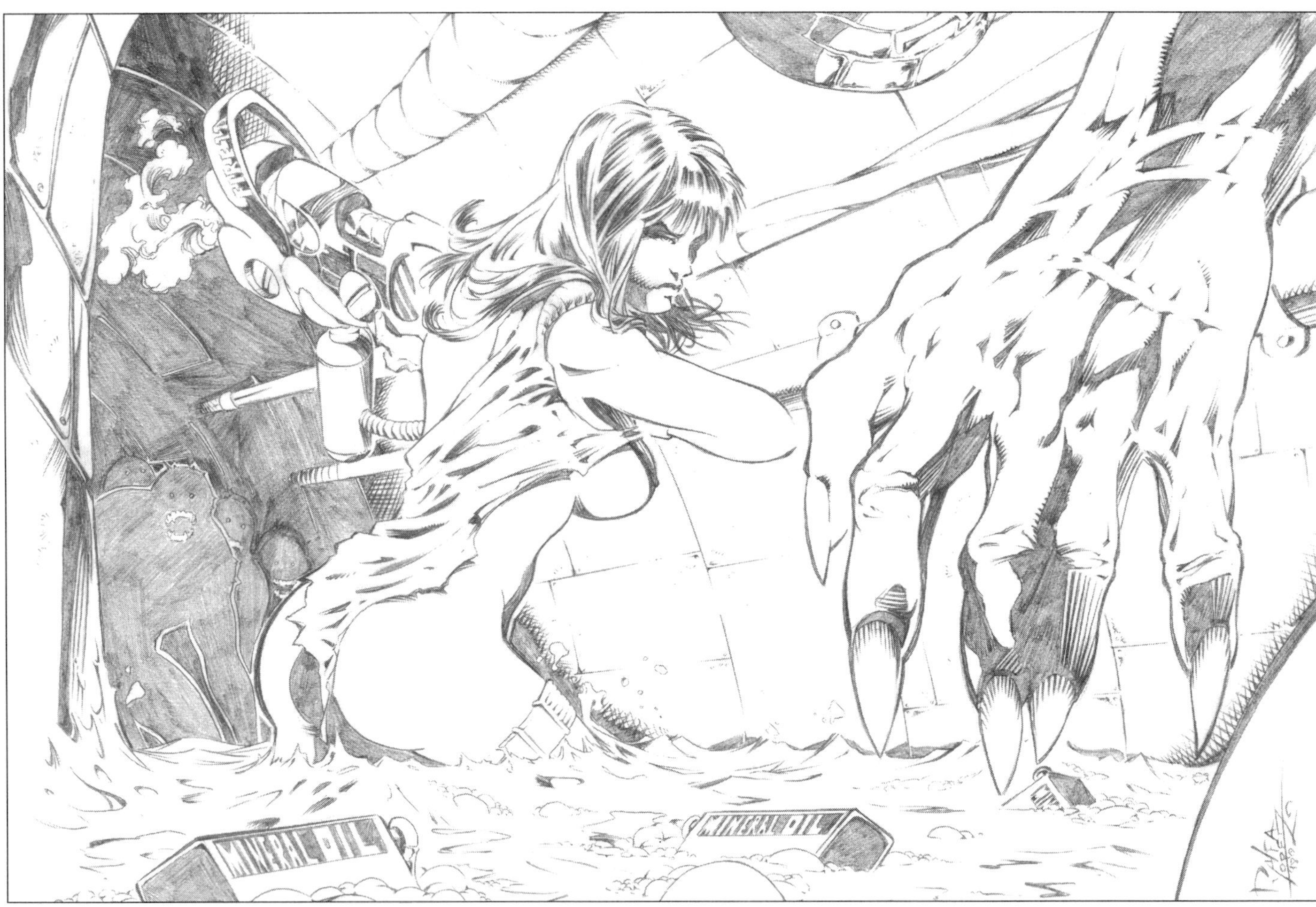

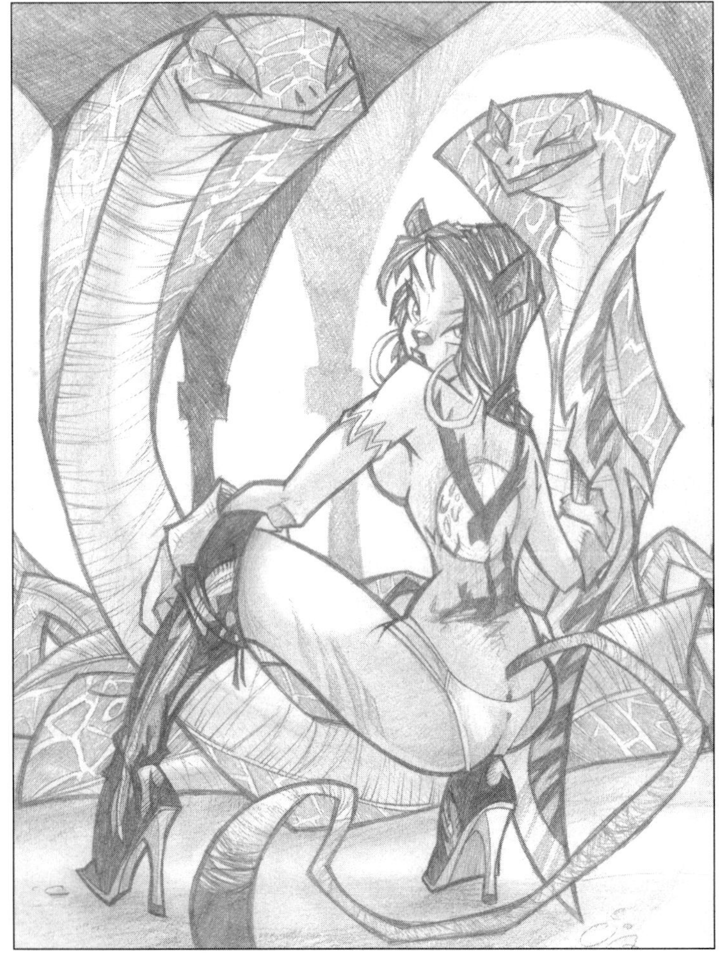

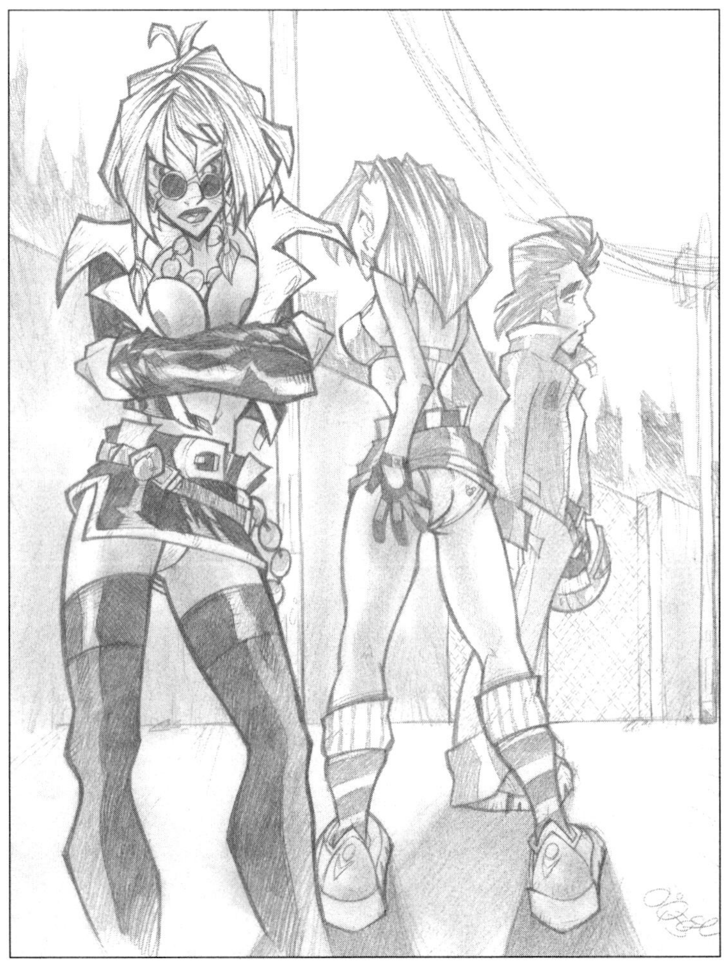

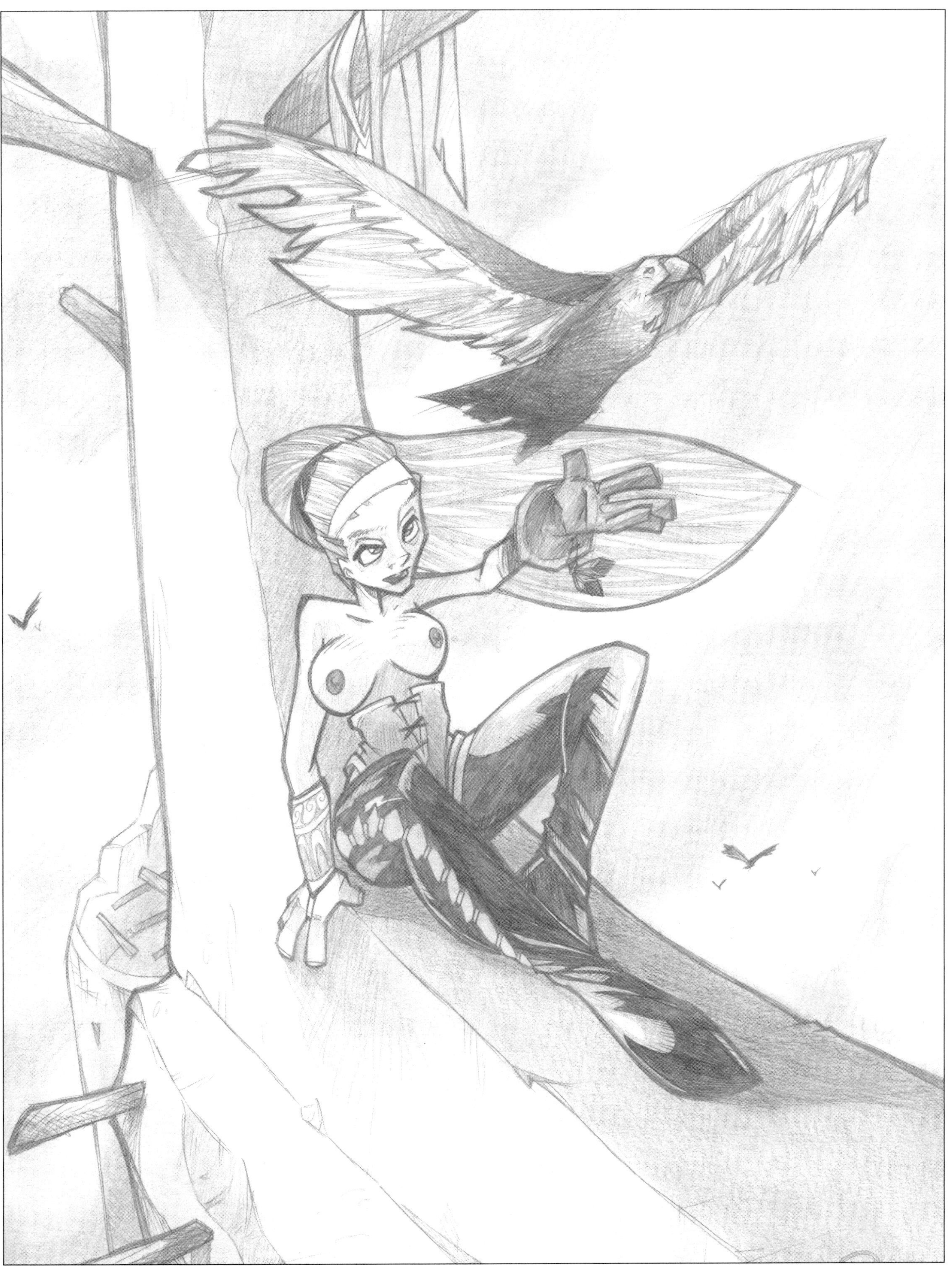

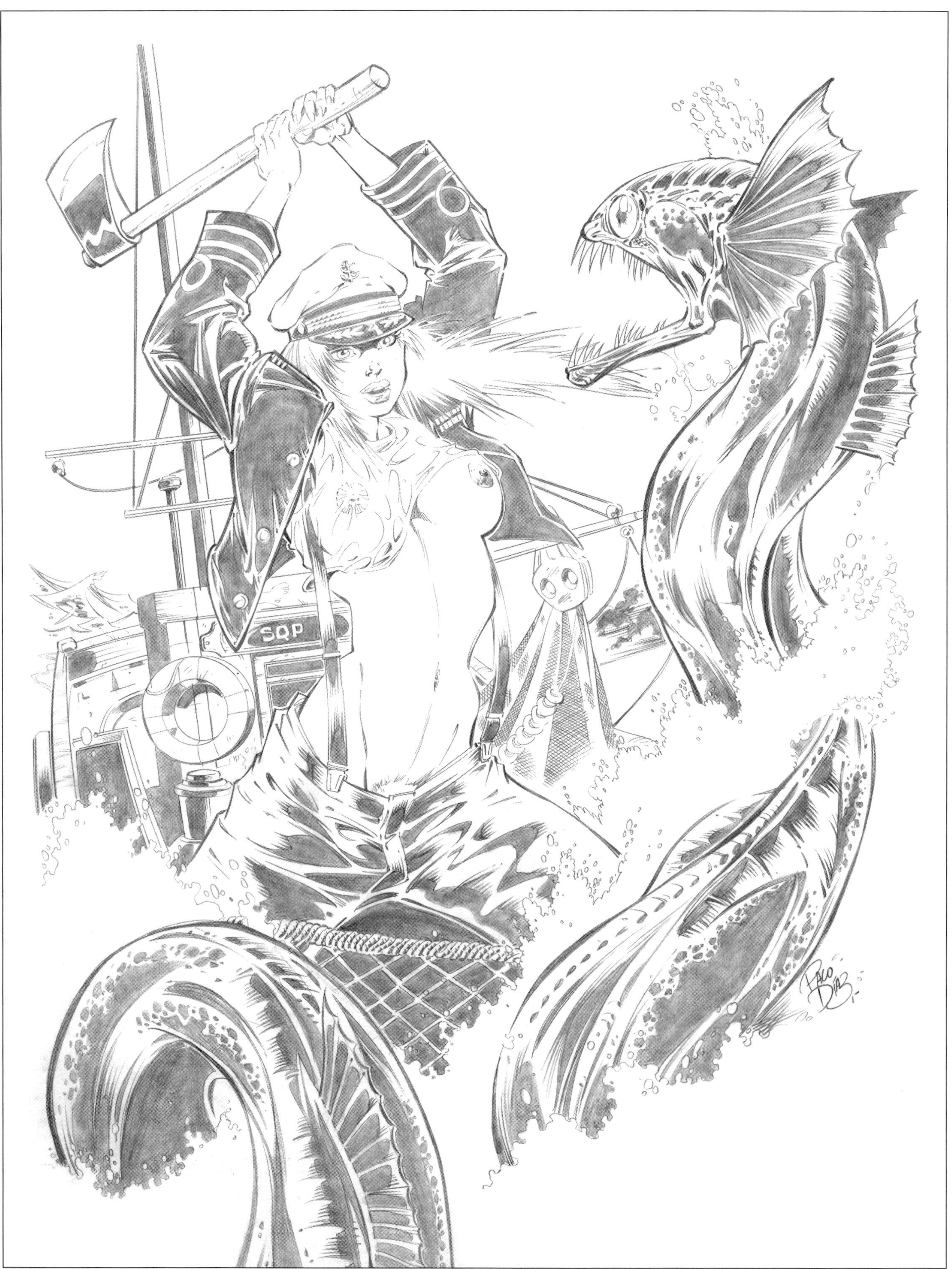
SQP

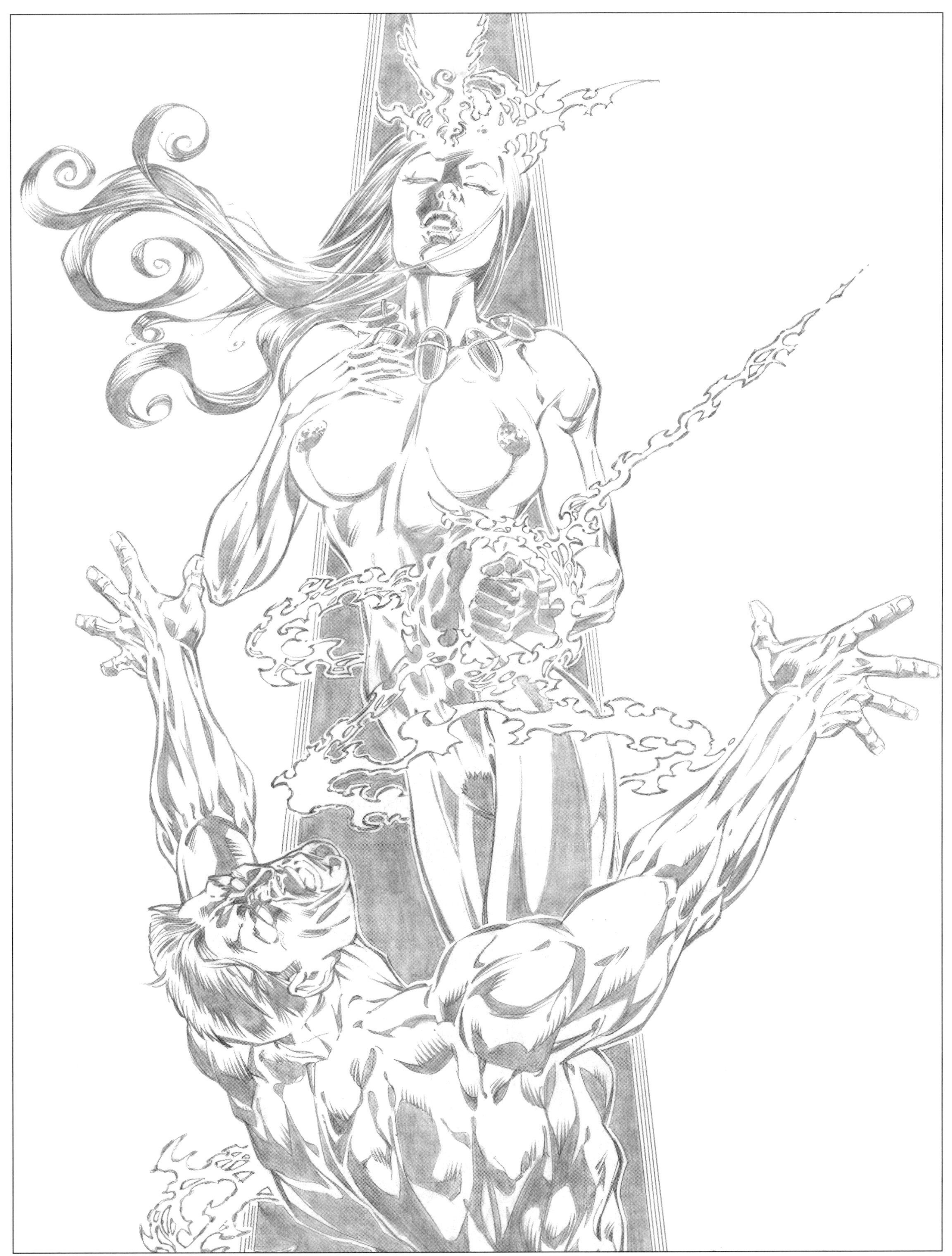

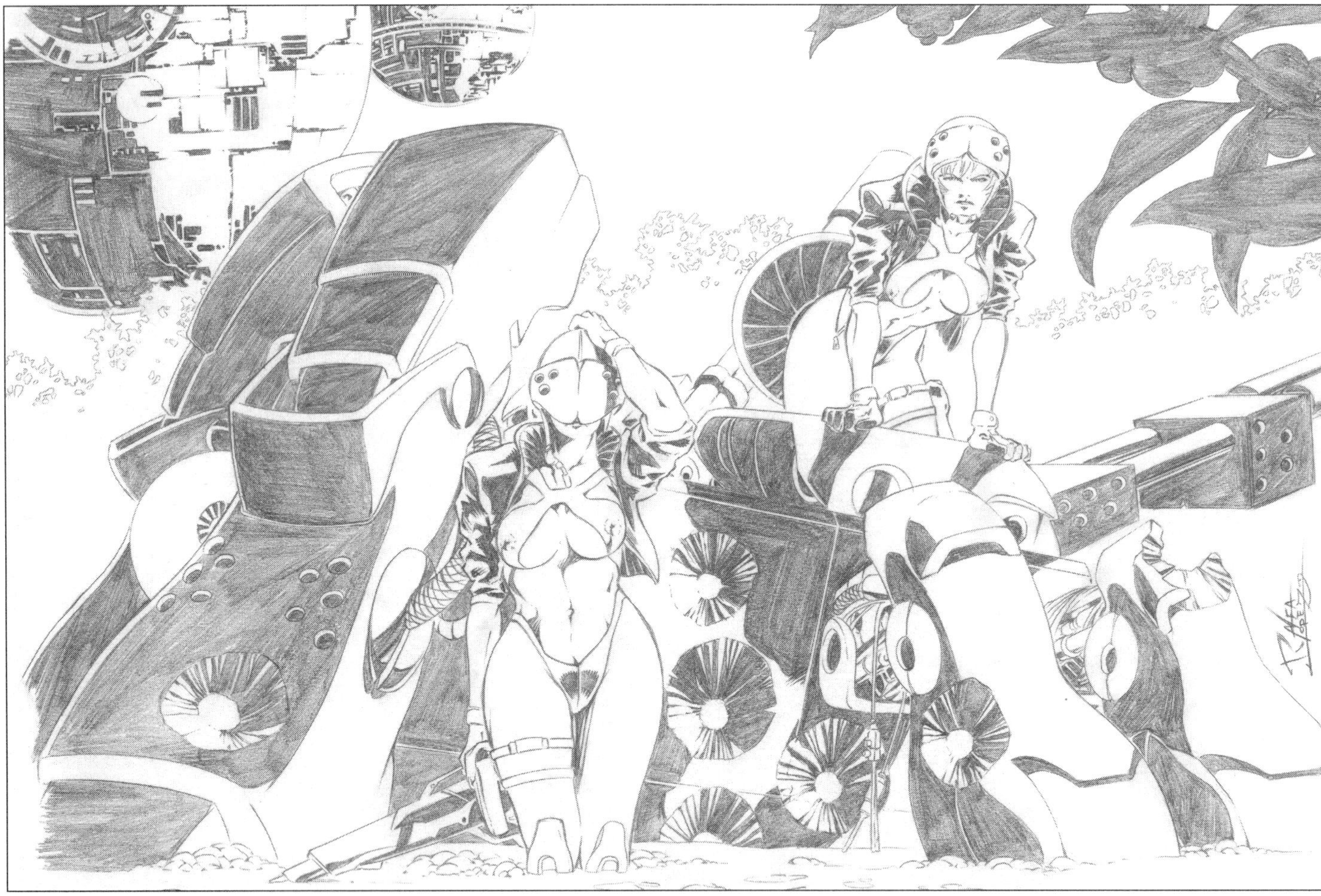

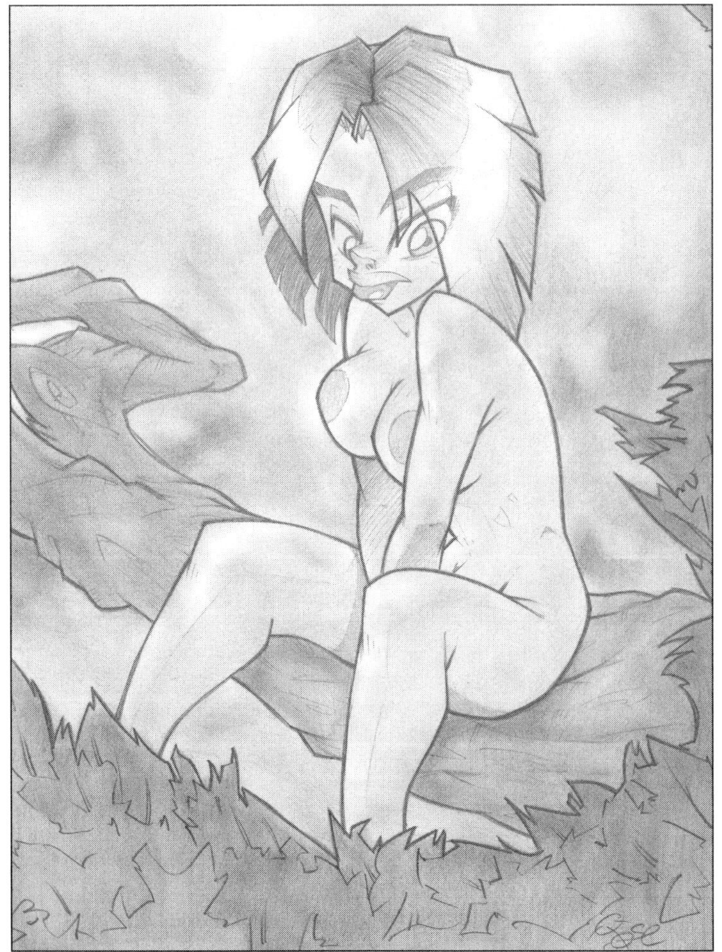

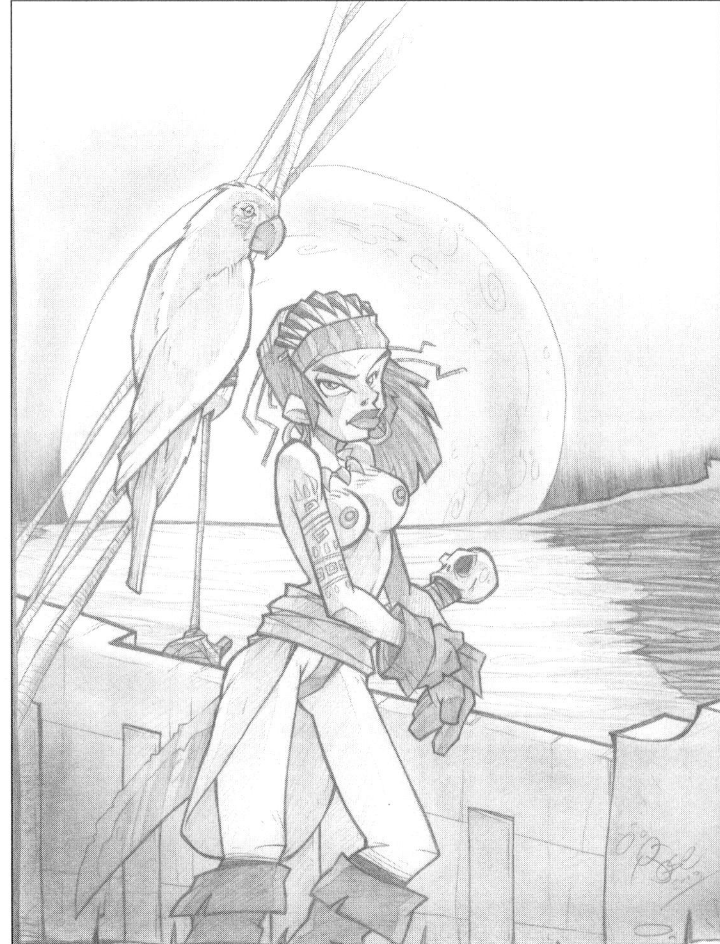

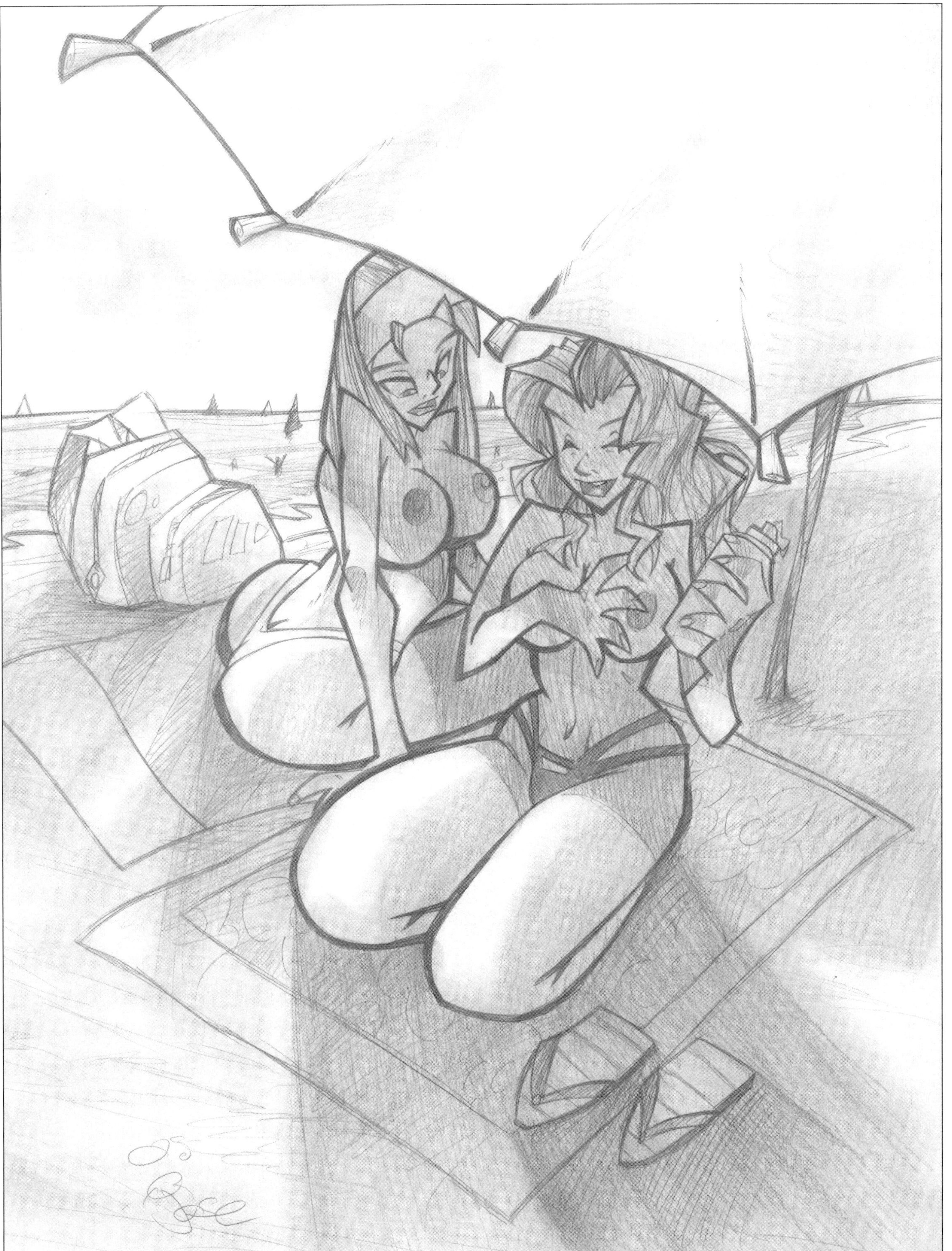

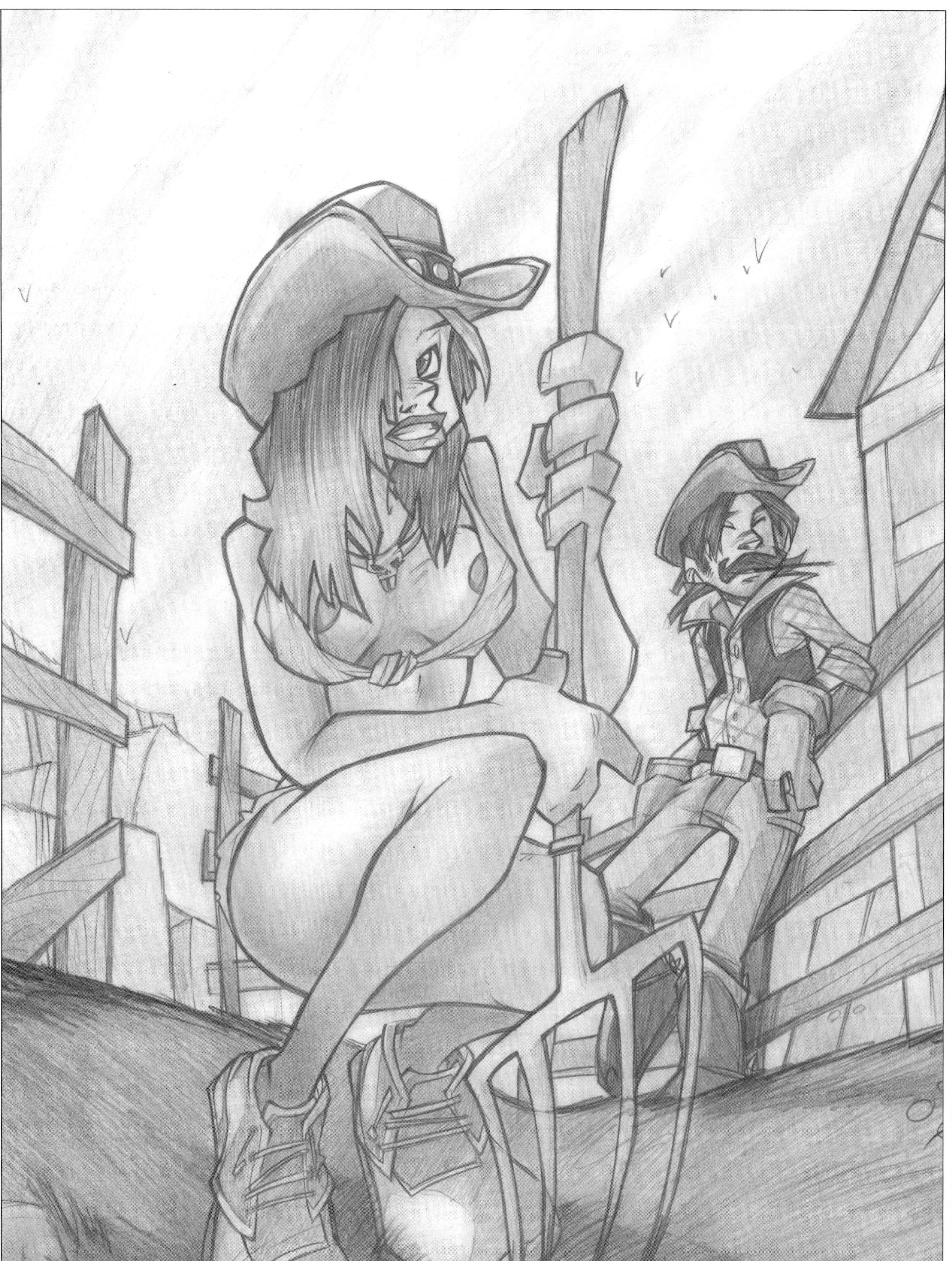

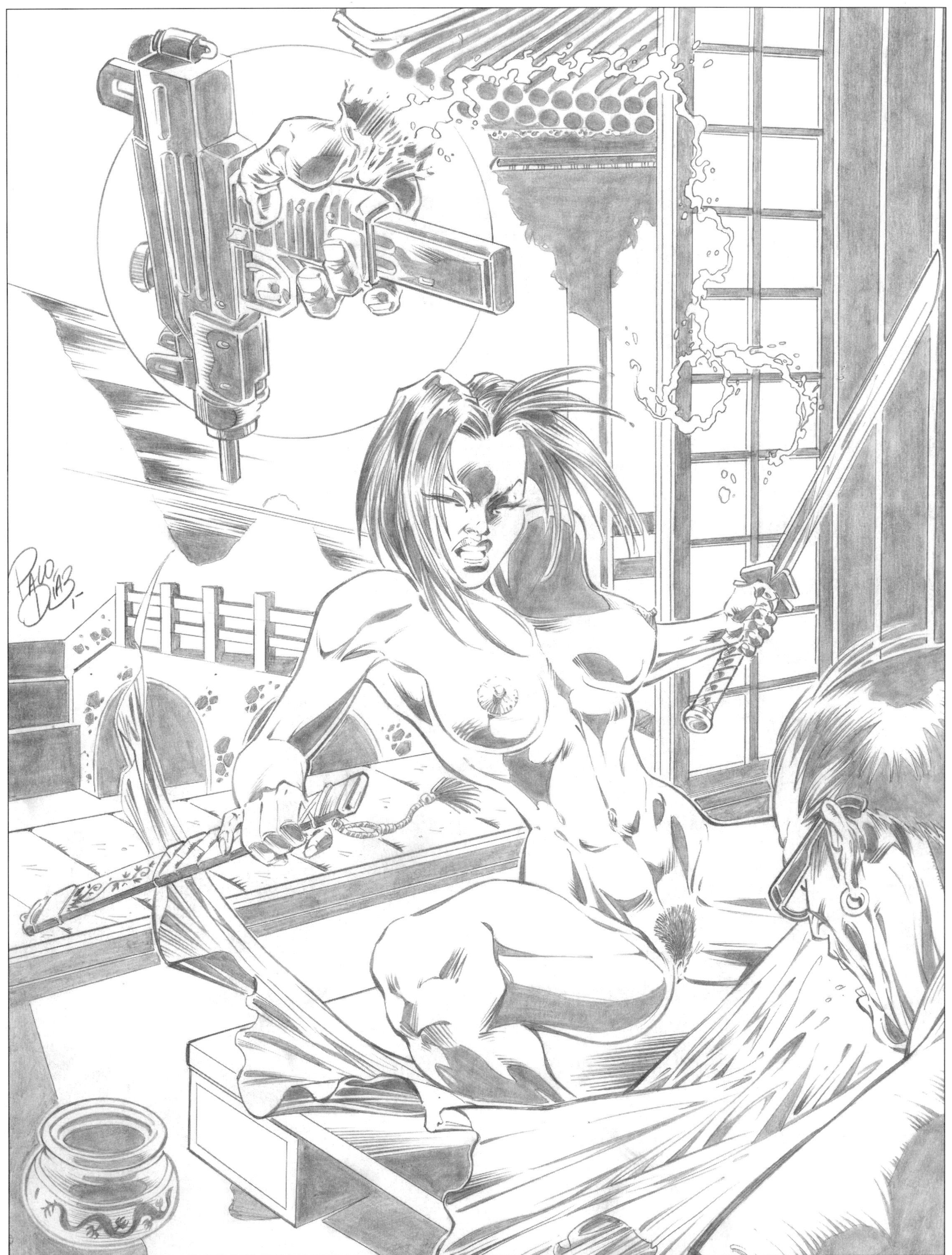

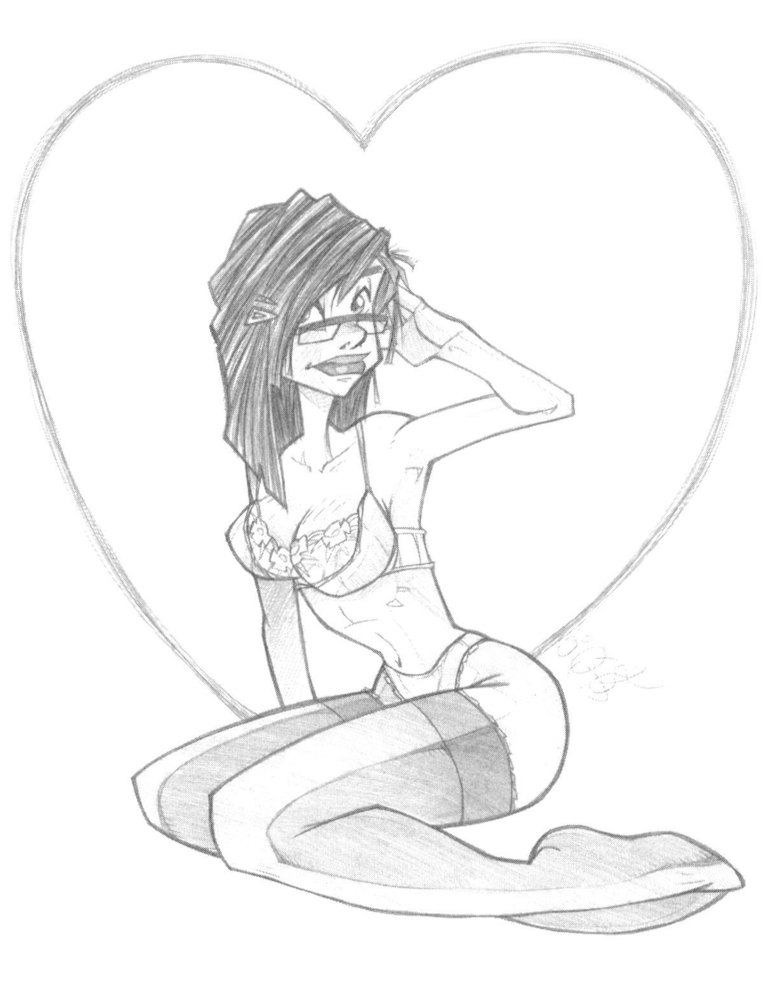

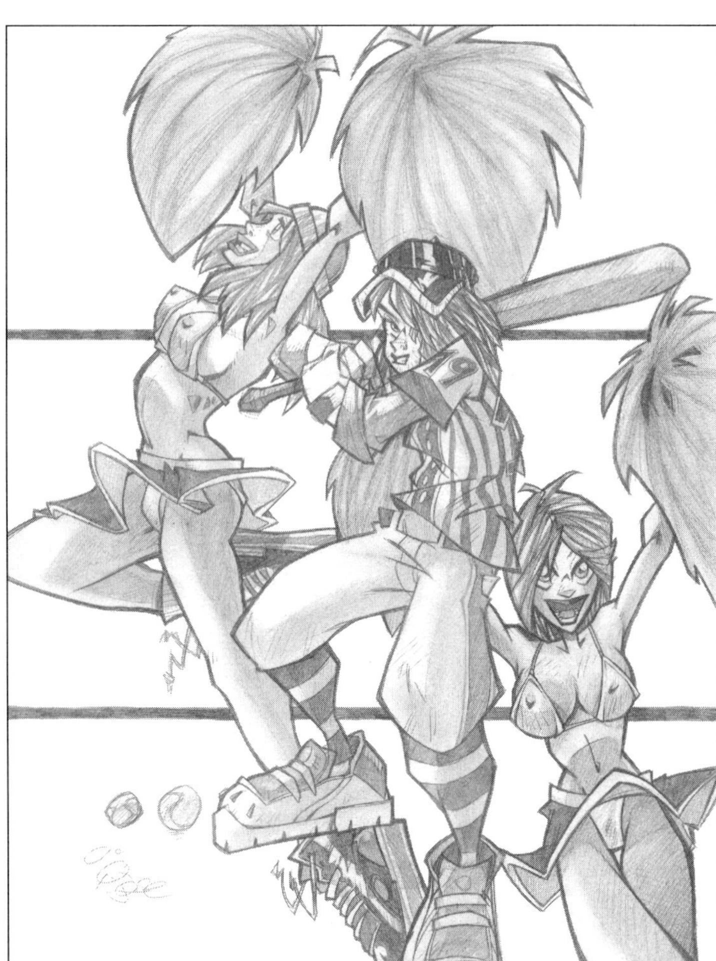

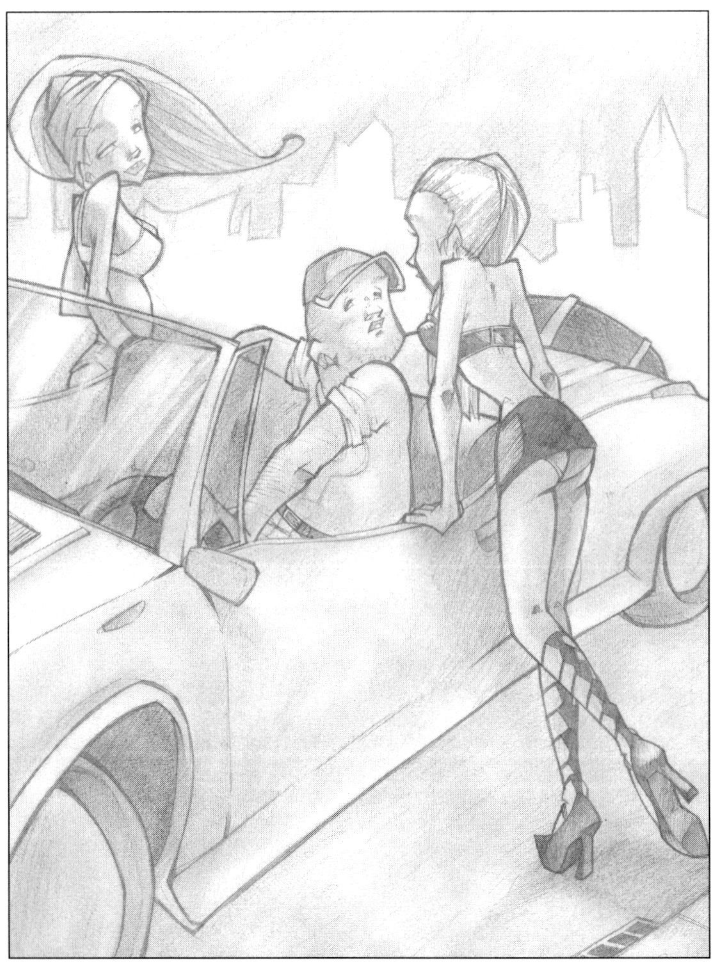

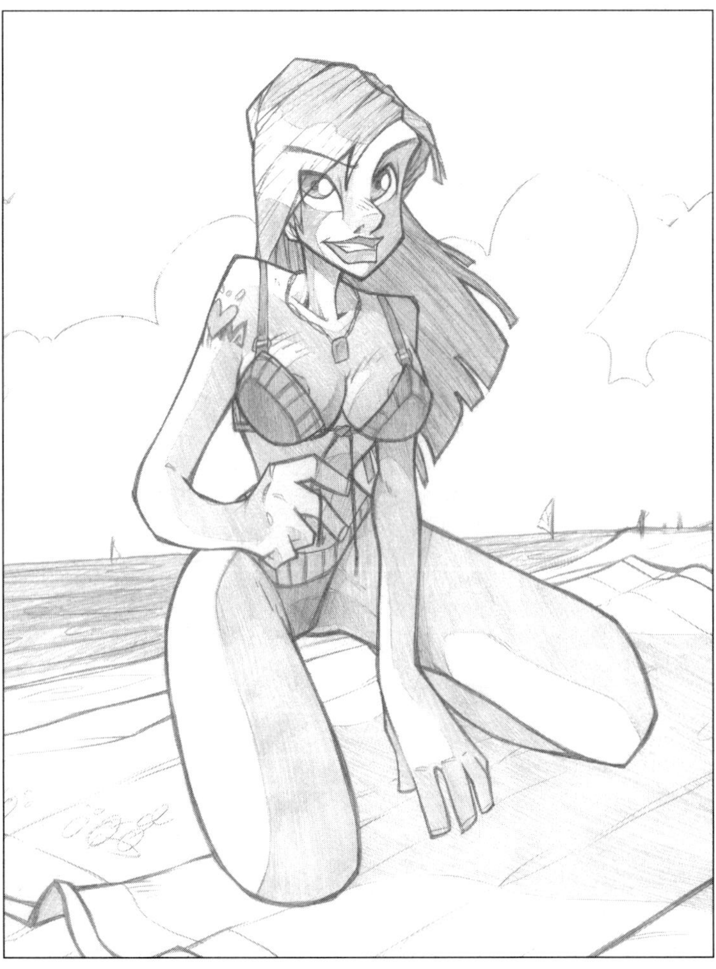

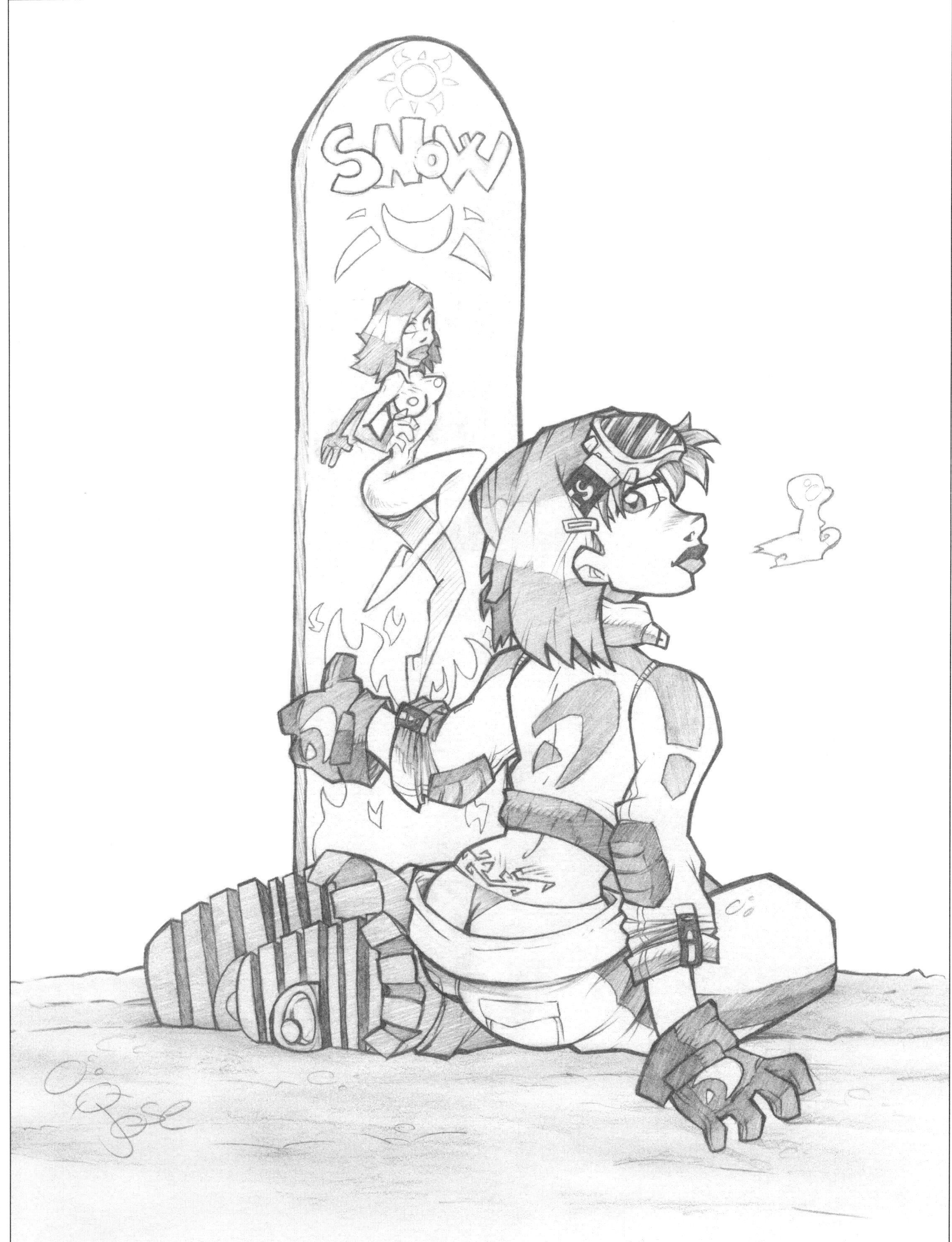
SNOW

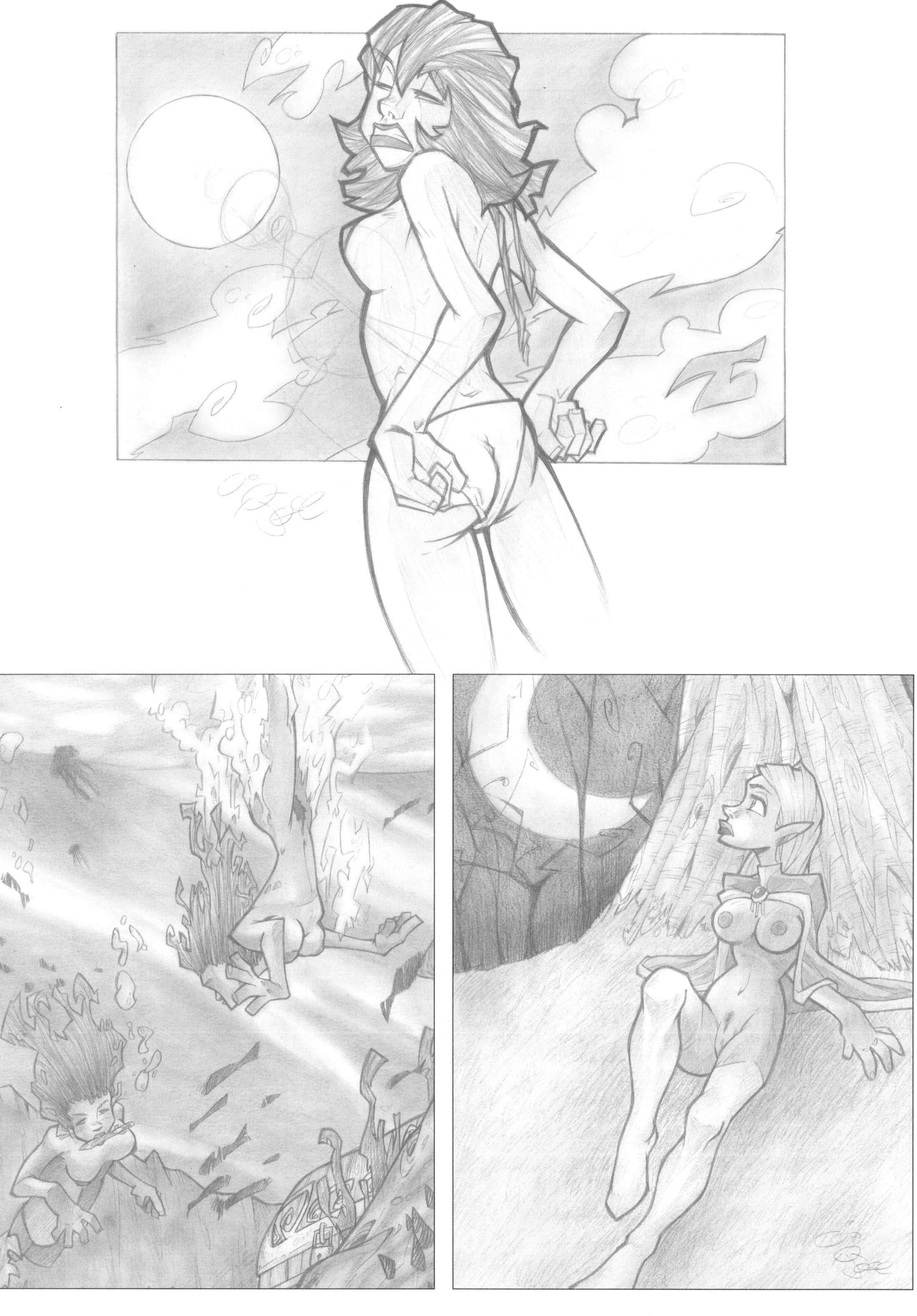

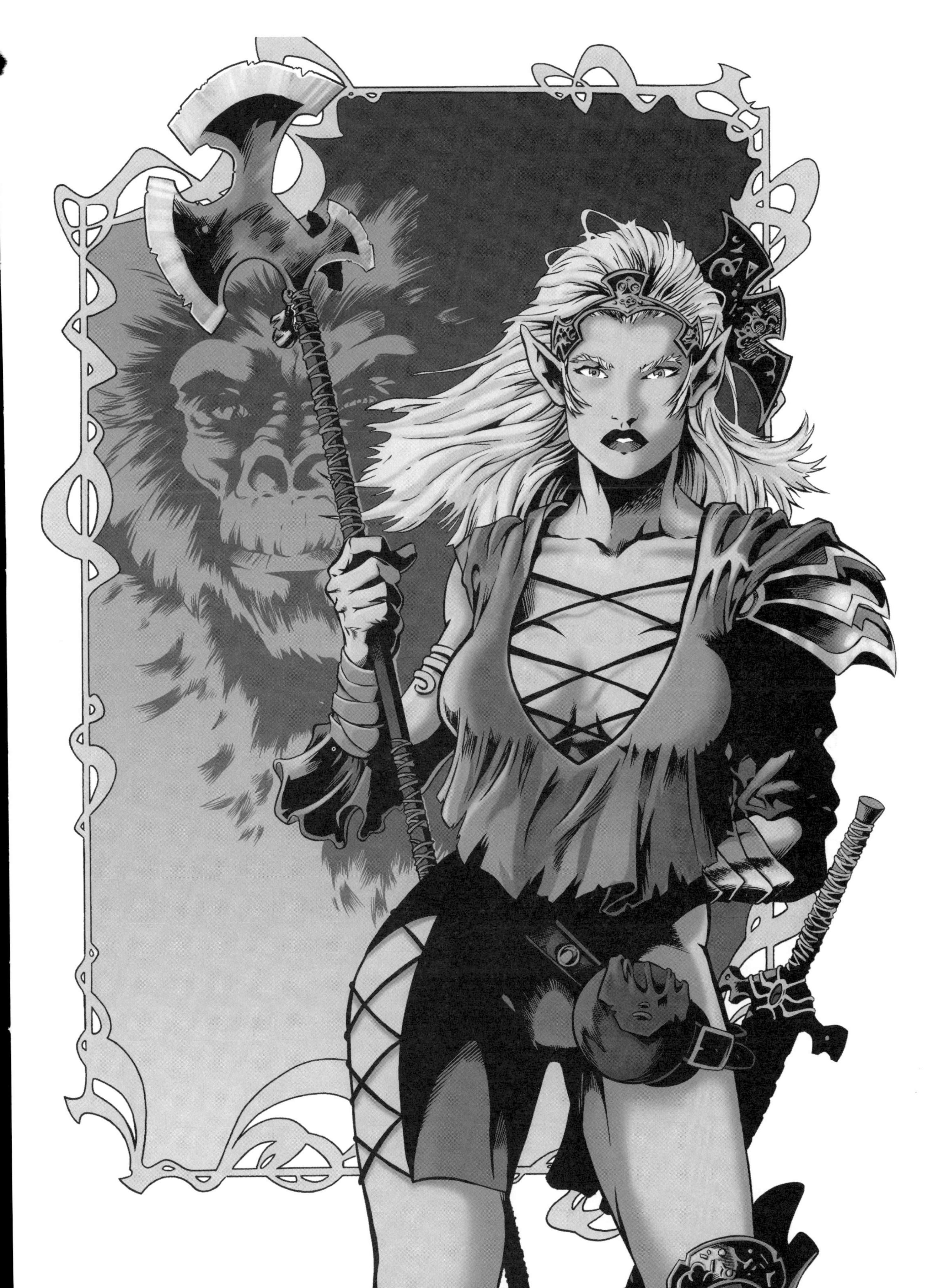

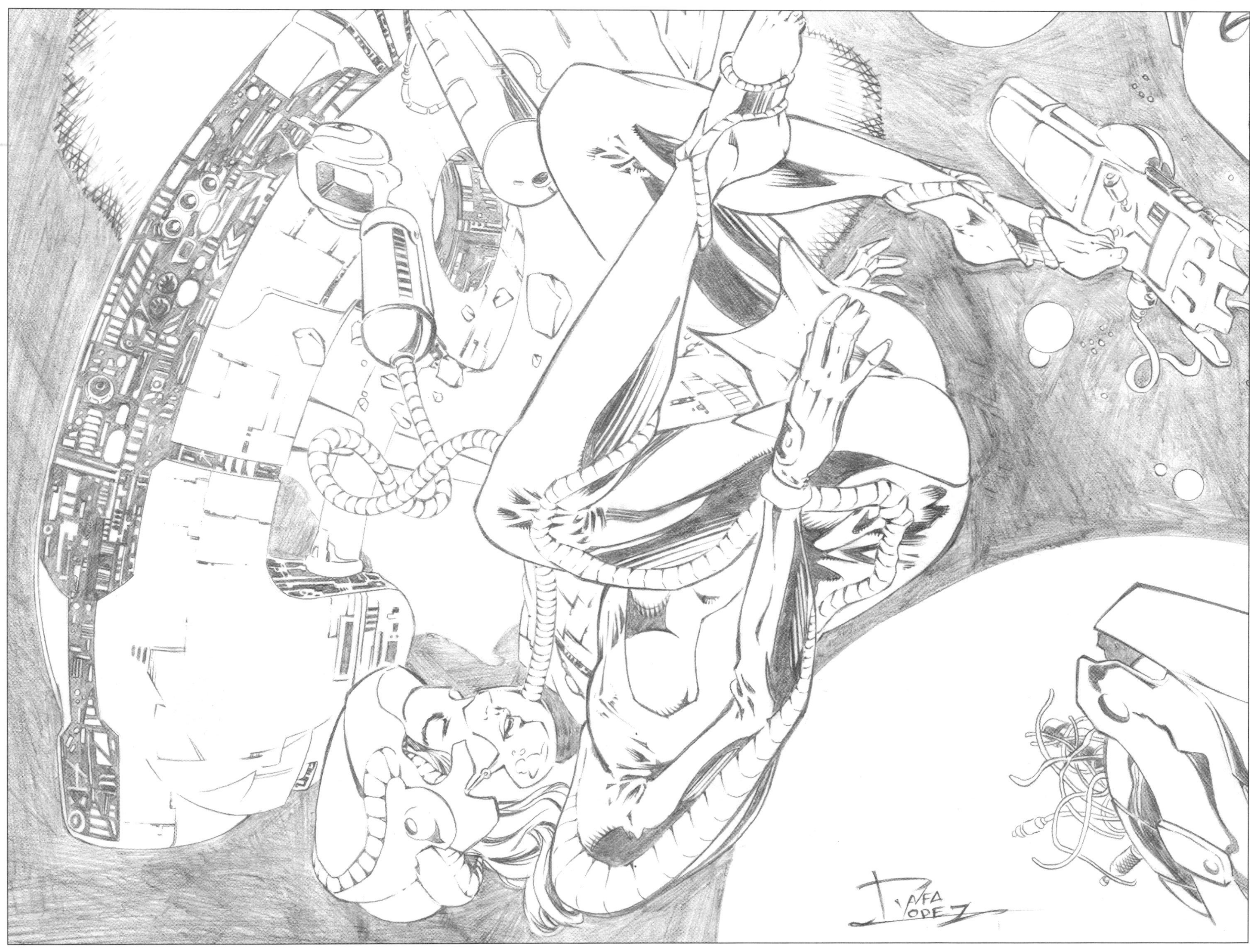
RAFA LOPEZ